THE FUTURE OF
LITURGICAL REFORM

by
J.B.M. FREDERICK
A.B., M.Div., Ph.D
Rector of Blechingley, Surrey

MOREHOUSE-BARLOW
78 DANBURY ROAD, WILTON, CT 06897

First published in Great Britain by Churchman Publishing Limited
Copyright © 1987 by J. B. M. Frederick
First American Edition published by Morehouse-Barlow, Wilton, Connecticut

Library of Congress Cataloging-in-Publication Data

Frederick J. B. M. (John Bassett Moore), 1930-
The future of liturgical reform.

1. Liturgics.   I. Title.
BV176.F74   1987   264'.009'04   87-24753

ISBN 0-8192-1412-4

Printed in the United States of America
by
BSC Litho, Harrisburg, PA

Contents

The Liturgical Movement

Changes in worship were meant to renew the Church. That hope enlisted the support, not only of scholars and technical specialists, but also the workaday clergy many of whom had a hand in it. The Liturgical Movement in the Roman Catholic Church achieved its greatest victories in the Second Vatican Council which enshrined its principles and opened the way for their widespread application. Many Anglicans, round the world, use modern words designed to speak for modern man in prayer. Scarcely a denomination exists which has not been deeply affected by reform in worship and moved by the underlying motif of spiritual renewal. Even those disposed by temperament or education to cherish 'traditional' forms were persuaded to up anchor in the service of a yet more ancient tradition where the faithful stood round the place of sacrifice offering goods they could clearly recognise to be their own, in gestures and words which spoke of daily experience. While some rejoiced to 'make liturgy' rather than to observe it, others with misgivings uttered subdued murmurings – something important had gone missing.

Against the pariahs, countercharges of medievalism, obscurantism or hardening arteries might be thrown; like Marxists, the reformers had confidence in their inevitable progress. The 1980 Alternative Service Book appears to some in England as the end of the matter – others take it as a pause in a never-ending process. But something has come adrift. On all sides we hear that the Liturgical Movement has run out of steam, that it has not filled the churches nor impressed the gospel on the rising generation. Among the convinced revisionists are to be found some elderly people impatient for change, while those most opposed include some young who are ardent traditionalists. Now however, we hear not just the detractors who miss the vision, but the reformers complaining of frustration. Misgivings are voiced by those who ought to be celebrating – but is not the Alternative Service Book widely accepted, the new American Episcopalian prayer book adopted by an overwhelming majority, the parish communion the norm in British Anglicanism? Maybe we had better take stock.

The Beginnings of Twentieth-century Liturgical Reform

Some people have an idea that the movement began in the Roman Catholic Church because of missionaries unhappy with latin. This was not the case – none of the lights of the movement was a missionary; they were mostly monks who lived in Belgium, France, Germany and Austria. Nor were they agreed on using the vernacular. What bothered Dom Lambert Beauduin of Mont César, father of the movement, was the contrast between the Church's dogmatic teaching about herself as the instrument of man's salvation, and the inadequate impressions conveyed by the Church at prayer.

> In the eyes of many, the liturgy is only a formal ceremony, a naive and superficial symbolism, an incomprehensible text, a religion-of-the-rite which ought to give over to religion of the spirit, a vague religious impression, an occasional element very secondary in the spiritual life. . .[1]

But the way for reform was prepared by one who would almost certainly have disliked the way it developed – Dom Prosper Guéranger. He restored the Benedictine abbey of Solesmes in 1832 and by his death in 1875 had enthroned a purified plainsong as the Church's official music. He enabled the monks to take part more fully in worship, shaping the views of the abbey at Beuron (restored 1868), its daughter houses at Mont César (Louvain), Maria Laach (1892, near Koblenz) and Maredsous (1872, Belgium), all of which played an important part in the later movement. True, he opposed the vernacular, did not aim for congregational participation, looked to the middle ages rather than to the early Church, failed to see the social ramifications of liturgical reform, hated local variations and rigidly suppressed them whenever he could, and was thoroughly authoritarian. But he got across to people an appreciation of the liturgy as the Church's public prayer having priority over the private devotions which then occupied the attention of most laypeople at mass. Whatever departures were made from his ideas and tastes, the later members of the Liturgical Movement were at one with him in wanting to exorcise the complications and corruptions of post-medieval Roman liturgy. Without Guéranger, the movement would not have developed when it did – he who would have disowned the movement, was indispensible to it. He showed that reform – and that meant change – was possible in the Roman Catholic Church.

When Beauduin addressed the Mâlines Congress of 1909, he aimed to put liturgy at the service of the parishes and, in calling attention to the liturgy's pastoral dimensions, he distinguished a motif marking out the movement henceforth. He was not to be deflected by any yearning for better forms but was intent on making the most of what was available and authorised.[2] In the publications issued by the houses of the Beuron congregation,[3] in the 'liturgical week' at Mont César in 1911 and at the lay conference at Maria Laach in Holy Week 1914, 'pastoral liturgy' meant two things. First, the liturgy binds men more closely to each other and to the Church where grace is available for man's healing. Secondly, the liturgy was understood to be a primary teaching tool. For the latter reason, there was a growing and unavoidable pressure in favour of the vernacular, however indifferent to it were the early protagonists of the movement.

Unlike the nineteenth-century Oxford Movement, the Liturgical Movement did not fall into two phases – academic and parochial – but always combined scholarship with popular writings and numerous clerical and lay conferences. The writings of the Berlin pastor Johannes Pinsk and those of Romano Guardini were backed up by the scholarship of Pius Parsch of the Augustinian monastery at Klosterneuberg near Vienna, J.A. Jungmann at Innsbruck University (see *The Mass of the Roman Rite*, English translation 1951), the Oratorians of Leipzig, Abbot Herwegen's periodical *Ecclesia Orans* and Casel's *Jahrbuch für Liturgiewissenschaft*. Beauduin published La Piété de l'Eglise in 1914 and his pupil Laporta wrote *Piété eucharistique* fifteen years later. In 1920 a liturgical institute was founded at Trier and in 1930 an International Liturgical Conference was held at Antwerp. The

3

curtailment by the Nazis of work among Young Catholic groups by people like Guardini, for example, forced the German Church to limit activities to liturgical gatherings – such meetings were apparently thought to be harmless – which, incidentally, brought home the idea of the liturgy as the heart of Christian community. The fruits of this phase were not spectacular – experimentation with 'dialogue masses' in Belgium and a bilingual ritual (book of occasional offices) in Austria in 1935. The movement did not enjoy general support in Germany and Austria and the authoritarian temper of Church life cast the innovators in the role of subversives.

The Effect of Papal Policy on Liturgical Development

The Papacy was drawn into a controversy it could no longer ignore. In 1940 the German bishops, unable to handle the disputes, appointed the first national liturgical commission which then issued directives allowing some chanting in German and the imposition of a commentator's voice reading a German translation of the celebrant's inaudible latin. Archbishop Grüber of Freiburg im Breisgau, Metropolitan of the Upper Rhine, denounced the movement's errors, and the apostolic nuncio then demanded the bishops do something. When the majority of the bishops came forward to protect the movement and the Archbishop of Vienna wrote to Rome refuting Grüber's complaints in detail, supported by the Cardinal Bishop of Breslau in April 1943 – in the name of all the other bishops – it was clear Grüber had overstated his case. (The papal Secretary of State, Cardinal Maglione, noted that Grüber had even objected to people saying Amen.) What Grüber deplored was presented as a gift to the bishops on Christmas Eve of 1943.

Clearly, Rome had been doing its homework – for some time in fact! The spirituality of Pius X (Pope 1903–14) had been informed with pastoral zeal and strong eucharistic piety one indication of which was the unusual desire to play down the cult of the Blessed Virgin.[4] His own experience as a parish priest had led him towards a flat rejection of the general view that non-liturgical cults were for the laity whilst the liturgy was for those specialists who could understand and perform it. As

4

choirmaster of the seminary at Padua and in his parishes, he disliked grandiose musical performances in church which employed the liturgy as a vehicle for impressive operatics. The motu proprio *Tra le Sollecitudini* of 1903 spelled the end of that era and was – be it noted – completely in accordance with Guéranger's teachings. In 1905 there followed the decree *Sacra Tridentina Synodus* encouraging daily lay communion. Participation – a characteristic of the movement throughout its later history – was the keynote, and it was not pure Guéranger:

> . . .in order to restore the true Christian spirit the faithful must be brought back to the first and indispensible source of that spirit, the active participation of the faithful in the sacred mysteries and in the public prayer of the Church.[5]

Five years later followed the decree *Quam Singulari* demanding an early age for first confession and first communion of children. Its aim was to restore an ancient practice and provide a lifelong sacramental experience.

By 1943, Pius XII had reached some conclusions of his own which, while not in the first instance liturgical, made adjudication of the liturgical disputes imperative in the Pope's eyes. His encyclical of 1943, *Mystici Corporis*, while concerned mainly with attacking a kind of mysticism which seemed to muddy the distinctions between Christ and the Church, the Head and the Body, took up the matter of the liturgy because that was the principal meeting-ground between Christ and the Body:[6]

> The body of the Church, discussed by his theologians in the encyclical on the Mystical Body, was for him no more than a projection of the Head [Christ], in the sense that, being shaped and conditioned by it, it can admit of but one manner of thinking, feeling, and acting. Hence his lack of understanding for any kind of pluralism, whether theological or disciplinary.[7]

In the forty years from 1903 the Papacy had developed the attitude that it had to intrude to ensure liturgical uniformity, particularly in the attitudes toward the liturgy itself, and it had also developed a pretty clear idea of just what participation in

5

liturgy ought to be like. When Rome moved, it found an ally ready to receive its decisive intervention – a flourishing Liturgical Movement which had reached similar attitudes towards liturgy.

In today's climate, when words like change and renewal are bandied about, we may easily fail to ask a basic question, an obvious and pressing question for those who have known only earlier days. Why was there a movement for Rome to embrace, at all? After all, earlier attempts had come to nought. One of these came to grief in the late eighteenth century when Bishop Scipione di'Ricci set forth reforms for his Tuscany diocese of Pistoia-Prato, a number of which sound familiar to us – one altar only in a church, no exposition of relics or flowers, no processions in honour of the Virgin or saints, no stations of the cross, no cult of sacred images (and especially no Sacred Heart) since these tended to distort or de-emphasise the eucharist. He wanted the vernacular and simplification of liturgy. He upheld receiving communion from the elements consecrated at the time rather than later from the reserved sacrament, lay bible reading, public liturgical responses by the people. In France, the Abbé Jube d'Asnières put forward similar reforms (described, no less, by Guéranger!)[8] – one altar used Sundays and feast days only and kept bare otherwise, the priest approaching the altar preceded by a large cross, the people answering in a loud voice, the people reciting nothing belonging to other ministers or choir, the elements brought forward at the offertory *ceremonialiter*, the fruits of the season brought to the altar, the chalice brought from the sacristy at the offertory without a veil, the canon said clearly and aloud. Missals, bible reading and the vernacular were encouraged. The upshot of all this – di'Ricci was accused of grave error in 1786 and deposed from his see in 1790; all similar reforms were condemned by the bull *Auctorem fidei* in 1794. So much for an eighteenth-century Liturgical Movement! The difference between 1794 and 1943 lies in two factors – papal involvement and the creation of a theological foundation for liturgical renewal broadly acceptable to the Roman Catholic Church. In Rome's eyes, the movement was the practical expression of a theology sympathetic to the Church's dogmatic and constitutional structure as well as a

6

means of enlisting the ordinary worshipper's active support for the Church's dogma and constitution. For that reason, the Papacy reconciled latin as 'the language of the universal church' to the need for the vernacular by providing for translations following the reading of the latin text, but not replacing it. That such an unwieldy procedure could be adopted – one later rejected – indicates clearly the papal priority of maintaining both one voice and local participation. Far from constituting a threat to church order, the movement received the papal blessing because its exponents had, from Beauduin right down the line, preached liturgy as the Church's servant, not her critic.

The Liturgical Movement's Triumph

French popularization of what Belgian pastoral instinct and German scholarship had made possible, was brought into full flower by the meeting of a number of Dominicans in a room of the publishing house Éditions du Cerf in Paris in 1943 giving birth in 1947 to the *Centre de Pastorale Liturgique* (CPL). Not only did this centre for publishing and conferences popularise the aims of the movement but it meant that for the first time it had a centre in a national capital and the backing of a national hierarchy. The movement's ideas were extensively promoted in Belgium, Holland, and even in Spain, by large and numerous conferences. And it had the backing of Rome. Abbé Michonneau's startling book *Revolution in a City Parish* showed the movement's principles applied in a parish and was widely read outside the Roman Catholic Church as well – inside the Roman Catholic Church it reached English readers as well as French.

The victory of the movement was proclaimed by the encyclical *Mediator Dei* of 1947. Some thought it a rap on the knuckles for liturgical innovators – these critics had failed to appreciate what had been happening in Rome since 1903. Apart from some censuring of those who would ruthlessly suppress extra-liturgical prayers and those who wanted to portray a celestial a-historical Christ (a somewhat mystifying reference), the brunt of the document is completely in line with the movement's, a point which the ageing Beauduin was quick to point out, calling it the liturgy's 'solemn charter'.[9]

Beauduin was not alone in his estimate of the encyclical. On 7 February 1958 Cardinal Montini addressed his archdiocese of Milan on liturgical education in a directive stressing the need to give the liturgical assembly the sense of a common action, the need to see, hear and understand (explicitly recognising Latin as a stumbling-block), and the need to see that participation requires activity. The future Pope of Vatican II, Paul VI, did not hesitate to insist on views indistinguishable from those of the Movement (nor to attribute them to Pius XII's lead).

For all its hierarchical frame of mind, *Mediator Dei* was a sort of hinge between a firm wall and a door which was soon to begin swinging noticeably. The firm wall was the teaching of Aquinas, regarded as definitive and authoritative in the teaching Church. The encyclical contained a significant paragraph:

> And there is no wonder that the faithful are accorded this privilege [offering sacrifice in the mass]: by reason of their baptism Christians are in the Mystical Body and become by a common title members of Christ the Priest; by the 'character' that is graven upon their souls they are appointed to the worship of God, and therefore, according to their condition, they share in the priesthood of Christ Himself.[10]

There are two notes in that wording: membership in the Mystical Body by baptism, and the imposition by baptism of a character on the soul by which the Christian is 'appointed to the worship of God'. We go right back to Aquinas:

> The whole Christian liturgy is derived from the priesthood of Christ. Hence it is clear that the character is particularly the character of Christ to whose priesthood the faithful are conformed by the sacramental character [i.e. those of baptism, confirmation and holy order]. These are nothing other than certain participations in the priesthood of Christ.[11]

In the first article of the question, Aquinas had stated that the sacraments are not only given for man's salvation, but also that by them (and particularly baptism) the faithful are deputed for divine worship. The impact of this is that the baptised have not only the 'character' which enables them to participate in Christ's priesthood, but the right to participate in Christian worship.

The encyclical's basis for the participation of the baptised in worship may go back to Aquinas, but how did it come about? People had revered Aquinas without reading in him the basis for the liturgical participation of the baptised! Once again we are thrown back to Beauduin. It was he who had seen in the lack of liturgical participation the consequences of individualism, the abandonment of prayer resulting from a desuetude of liturgy, the common view of the hierarchy as a legalistic administration. He it was who pushed the liturgy in a pastoral setting as the basis of a 'piety solid, healthy, abundant, and truly catholic', requiring participation by all the faithful.

> The fundamental theme of active participation, supplied by Pius X, served to crystalise Dom Beauduin's aspirations and to sustain his efforts. The active participation of the faithful, which was one of the first *leitmotive*, was no recent formula: it was founded on the conception of the Church as Body of Christ; the members of the Church have the right to take part actively in the sacrifice of the mass.[12]

Pius X, however, had not recovered Aquinas. It was Beauduin who steeped himself in Aquinas and whose writings were said to have much influenced the relevant passage in the 1947 encyclical.

We said the encyclical was a kind of hinge. The door began to move appreciably at the Second Vatican Council. Here the role of CPL was vital, because it forged a common front between the French and German schools, a common view which was necessary if the Council was to act. The Constitution on the Sacred Liturgy took up the revived aspect of Aquinas; it said that the Christian people's participation in liturgy 'is their right and duty by reason of their baptism' (p.14). Then the Constitution laid down principles for liturgical reform derived from this understanding of participation: liturgy pertains to all the faithful and each rank and office has its own way of participating which must be safeguarded and enhanced; all who take a leading part in the liturgy must be 'deeply imbued with the spirit of the liturgy', communal rites are preferred to 'the individual and quasi-private'; and every care is to be taken to encourage the 'active participation' of all the baptised (caps. 23–32).

If *Mediator Dei* was traditionally hierarchical in the accepted sense, the ecclesiology of Vatican II marks a considerable change of emphasis. In the Dogmatic Constitution on the Church there appear headings like 'On the People of God', 'On the hierarchical structure of the Church and in particular on the Episcopate', and 'The Laity'. The encyclical had been careful to stress that priests are set 'in a class apart from all other Christians who are not endowed with this super-natural power (to offer sacrifice)'; the emphasis is on the priest's individual 'character', on his power in individualistic terms. Vatican II's documents involved considerable discussion of the relations between Pope and the episcopal college and the emphasis was on their acting in concert; it was even stated that bishops have their own area of competence and are not to be regarded as vicars of the Pope. The laity were considered as an order within the Church. Within this setting, the effect was to tone down attention to the priest's 'character'.

Certain other points in the Constitution on the Sacred Liturgy are worth noting. Baptism and eucharist are coupled in discussion (cap. 6) and the term 'liturgy' is applied principally to a baptismal-eucharistic unity(cap. 10). Second, the diffusion of authority throughout the episcopal college takes a practical and liturgical form in allowing local bishops to regulate usage, subject to overall papal control(caps. 22 & 26), a change from *Mediator Dei*'s insistence that the vernacular can only be allowed as an exception to the general rule and only on papal authority(Para. 64). Third, in line with this, guidelines are laid down for adapting liturgical usage to local needs (caps. 37–40). But the key word is participation. This explains why, *pace* remarks about preserving latin (cap. 36), the bishops were quick to abandon it.

A year after the Council, the decree *Inter Oecumenici* made reforms implementing the principles as mandatory. What *Mediator Dei* had proclaimed on behalf of Rome, the decree solemnised for the every part of the Roman Catholic Church.

10

Symbolically, the decree's date was 25 January 1964 – the Feast of the Conversion of St Paul. From then on revisions were rapid – in 1969 new orders for baptism, burial and marriage; from 1968–72 new ordination rites; an interim liturgy in 1964 and in 1969 a new order for mass. In earlier days, worshippers were encouraged to participate in the conviction that they would serve to reinforce the Church's accepted hierarchical structure. Now a fascinating change was occurring. Lay activity in liturgy implied lay activity elsewhere too. The liturgy was beginning to press the shape of the Church to conform to the liturgy's pattern of the Church. Considering the similarities between post-Tridentine liturgy and Church structure, that ought to have surprised no one. But it has taken many by surprise who ought to have known better. Nor have we heard the last of it yet.

The Liturgical Movement in Anglicanism

The story of the Liturgical Movement in Anglicanism has a different feel to it. In the first place, the need for reform of worship did not seem so pressing as in Rome, not at least to Anglicans – revision perhaps, but hardly reform. One of the disadvantages of taking pride in the Reformation is the temptation to believe the Church has already had its *aggiornamento*. Not only had the vernacular (or something approaching it) been in use since 1549 – and a much-prized standard of English at that – but there had been revisions in 1552 and 1662. Secondly, the revisions had little to do with modernization or with language, apart from some updating of the psalms, they were adjustments between schools of churchmanship, part of the unending process of reckoning with tensions between Anglicanism's catholic and protestant traditions. That history is well known. While the 1928 prayer book was ostensibly proposed for the sake of modernization, it was scuppered by parties who were far more interested in what they saw as adverse changes in the balance of doctrine. Thirdly, familiar language was retained not from simple nostalgic reasons but because the existing language was itself useful – its use had become a necessary art practised for the sake of the Church's peace. It was downright dangerous to play about with that language whose studied ambiguities allowed the churchmanship schools freedom.

11

'Sacrifice of praise and thanksgiving' in the communion service could refer to a genuine eucharistic sacrifice in the catholic sense, or it could mean that the only sacrifice was of praise. Judging by the 1928 book, England had had no twentieth-century Liturgical Movement. And the same was true for overseas Anglicans – revisions were adaptations to local requirements, as the prefaces to the American books plainly state. Fourthly, no official system such as Casel's mystery theology had been devised to propel an Anglican movement. The hierarchy did not feel moved to enforce order in the theological jungle nor was there a corresponding desire to bind worshippers more closely to the hierarchy by means of the liturgy (an objective clearly in Beaduin's mind) – that would not have been a very Anglican thing to do. Prayers expressing a conscious filial dependence on bishop and pope seemed appropriate to the Roman rite but we can hardly imagine Anglicans treating their bishop, the Church Assembly/General Synod and Lambeth Conference with that sort of deference! Lastly, no central authority like the papacy voiced a new spirit in liturgy, hence voluntary societies like Parish and People assumed enormous importance for the movement. Authorities in the Church of England remained for some time uninterested – probably still fatigued by the frustrating memories of the 1928 debacle. The keynote document *Towards the Conversion of England* published to outline the Church's strategy in the post-Second World War era, was entirely unconcerned with liturgy and ignored the subject.

Whatever impetus was felt for liturgical reform stemmed from three sources – development of emphases already present in the prayer book, a pragmatic and piecemeal appropriation of such mystery theology as could be digested by Anglicans, and the search for early Christian norms in order to undercut the rows over churchmanship by going behind the quarrels to prior times.

The foremost and most successful springboard for reform came with the Parish Communion movement which illustrates the appeal of prayer book rationale on its own. Rather like spelling out the implications of the decrees of Vatican II, the Parish Communion adherents tried to explicate the implications of text and rubric for the centrality of the eucharist, 'the Lord's own service on the Lord's own day'. The wellknown liturgist-historian Frere called it 'the way of the prayer book'.[13] A future Archbishop of Canterbury, Cosmo Gordon Lang (when Bishop of Stepney) first talked of the Parish Communion but Evangelicals were cool to the idea when it was put to Convocation in 1906. They showed an attitude to the prayer book similar to Anglo-Catholics – the book contained a wide range of items amongst which to pick at will, but they were not going to be bound closely by rubrics arbitrarily elevated into theological principles. Whatever the rubrics might say, whatever practice had been normal in the early sixteenth century, no demonstration had been worked out on a non-partizan basis as to why the Sunday eucharist had to replace matins everywhere. For example, despite attacks on the theological issues by Hebert and Hicks, the sacrificial aspect of eucharist continued to be opposed to the meal aspect – the tools for seeing the meal as sacrificial only became available with writers like the Roman Catholic Louis Bouyer. Prayer book teaching could not of itself deal with the matter. The Parish Communion only took hold in the 1950–60s by which time other influences had come into play. The writings of Colin Buchanan and the Grove Books Press, centred on St John's Theological College, Nottingham, reveal that teachings from outside the prayer book later engaged the active support of Evangelicals for the Liturgical Movement. For all his emphasis on the prayer book – or reading between the lines aided by medieval texts – Percy Dearmer's *The Parson's Handbook*, widely read well beyond his death in 1936, never could have provided a theological foundation for liturgical reform. The one great advantage of churchmanship squabbles in the Church of England was that they forced adequate eucharistic rationale to be produced from outside the familiar terms of the essentially medieval prayer book.

Meanwhile, Anglicans were becoming aware of what was going on in the Liturgical Movement on the continent. From 1925, the journal *Theology* invited short reviews by French Benedictines. Friedrich Heiler's *The Spirit of Worship* (1926) reflected the movement's teachings. *Parish and People* made full use of *La Maison-Dieu* (published by CPL in Paris) and, in advocating the 'westward' position of the celebrant, specifically credited the French publication for its data. As early as 1935, Hebert popularised thinking from the continent in his *Liturgy and Society* which aimed at three objectives: an understanding of the Church as the mystical body of Christ, a constructive biblical critique of liberal theology, and the mission of the Church to the modern world.[14]

An individual example of influence from the movement on the continent is J.O. Cobham, one of the post-Great War crop of English ordinands. When he entered Corpus Christi College, Cambridge in 1919, he found that the New Testament scholar E.C. Hoskyns as Dean of the chapel and the Tutor, Will Spens, had ordered the services so that matins was said Sunday at 8 a.m. followed by a sung eucharist at 8:30 o'clock. Subsequently, college members used to gather in each others' rooms for breakfast. Hoskyns influenced Cobham to sit under Heiler and Rudolf Otto at Marburg in 1923 where he also attended Bultmann's lectures. Like Hoskyns, Cobham reflected the desire to find a scripture-based authority within the Church to undercut the churchmanship divisions. Having paid a week's visit at Maria Laach at Heiler's urging in 1924, Cobham went to Westcott House, Cambridge, finding at that theological college an 8:30 a.m. Sunday eucharist and an enthusiastic Vice-Principal and lecturer on the history of liturgy, E.C. Ratcliff. Following a curacy in Winchester, Cobham returned to Westcott House as Vice-Principal and became Ratcliff's successor as lecturer on liturgy. Becoming Principal of the Queen's College, Birmingham in 1934, we see the clear operation of the 'back to patristic sources' urge in that he managed to delay the building of a college chapel until 1939 when he had established sufficient trust in him by the College Council to allow him to build a chapel on distinctly Liturgical Movement lines, and to introduce a 'patristic ceremonial'.[15] In turn this rite became the basis of an SPCK film strip in 1953[16] an illustration from which appeared in Basil Minchin's influential book *The Celebration of the Eucharist Facing the People*. The patristic motif appeared again when, as Archdeacon of Durham, he advised the vicar of St Cuthbert's, Peterlee (a former pupil of his) to build a church with a 'basilican ground plan' similar to Q.C.B.'s. Similar use of early Christian models was evident in A.H. Couratin's text for Series 2 (based on Hippolytus) – he had also been in Durham with Cobham. Experimentation became more general on 'early' lines – Southcott at Halton, Leeds, Robinson and Moule at Clare College, Cambridge, and the Birmingham trio of Cope, Davies, and Tytler on Independent Television in 1959.

The Anglican old-boy net was beginning to operate in favour of the Liturgical Movement – lines from the universities (particularly Cambridge [17]) and theological colleges criss-crossing. If we consider the sixteen contributors to *The Parish Communion* in 1937, we find that of the fourteen who were university graduates eight were from Cambridge including three who were at Corpus. Two had served together in the same parish, two others had taught at the same missionary college. Some of these (like H.H.V. de Candole, co-author with Couratin of *Re-Shaping the Liturgy*, a product of Westcott House, and a contributor to *The Parish Communion*) became members of the Archbishop's Liturgical Commission formed in 1954, which was adopted for the Church by the General Synod in 1971. The Alternative Service Book of November 1980 is, to date, the crowning achievement of the Commission and was followed by a revision of Lent and Holy Week rites in 1984.

A unique contributor to liturgical reform was Dom Gregory Dix of Nashdom whose monumental tome *The Shape of the Liturgy* adorns many parsons' shelves. He drew attention to early Christian sources and made entertaining observations on the less convincing aspects of churchmanship controversy, but he stood outside the movement, working in virtual isolation from contemporary scholars, intruding like a bolt from the blue into discussions with erudite bits of 'evidence from liturgical sources'. His conclusions were not always sound but his invaluable achievement was to take liturgy seriously from a perspective of sympathy and toleration, blowing away some of the cobwebs.

2

Impasse for Reform

Has the Liturgical Movement been a success? Have its objectives been fulfilled and if so, is that enough? These questions lead us to examine the rationale underlying the movement – Casel's mystery theology. Casel took St Paul to mean by 'mysteries' not just what lies beyond comprehension, but God's plan as it stood unveiled in Christ, a plan whereby we enter the threefold mystery of God – the mystery of God in himself (into which no man can enter lest he die), the mystery of Christ, i.e. 'the mystery in person, because he shows the invisible godhead in the flesh',[1] and the mystery of Christ's actions as those shine through the sacraments. Above all, the mystery of Christ was seen not as hidden teaching, but as saving events. Casel was convinced Christians deal with no abstract realities called salvation or eternal life *contained* by events. In writing of Romans 6:2 ('We died to sin . . . Have you forgotten that when we were baptized . . . we were baptized into his death?'), he emphasised it is necessary to die with Christ. Baptism is participation in one particular death, the saving death of Christ which brings new life. The Church is part of the mystery of Christ, not simply because it is the community which remembers these saving acts, or even because the Church reaps the benefits of that death, but because in the sacraments the saving events are themselves made present in the Church's sacramental acts. By doing what the Lord did, the Church makes his acts present in a sacramental manner. The sacraments do not repeat these historical happenings, nor do they add to them, nor do they simply apply the saving effects of the past events; for Casel, the sacraments re-present the events themselves so that the believer experiences the events. The sacraments realise the very saving acts of God which occurred in Palestine. The actions of the liturgy are the historical events of our salvation made sacramentally present – they are not two actions, past

16

and present, which become one. Never content with worship as a mental recollection designed to benefit the soul by encouraging good dispositions through prayer and the imitation of Christ's virtues, he sought to clarify the Catholic contention that sacraments bridge a time gap. In the sacraments the worshipper is brought to the Christ-events themselves and he appropriates their benefits partly by grace infusing these events' contents into the soul and partly by being transported to the events through a sacramental enactment believed to realise what is symbolised. The worshipper at mass is present at Calvary and the sacrament is relied on to obliterate the limitations of time; the newly baptised person has just died and been raised to new life with his Lord; the penitent who hears the priest's absolution is, for all intents and purposes, hearing the forgiving voice of Jesus himself.

The time gap separating the faithful from Christ's actions is a problem to be solved and the task of the sacraments is to jump that gap, incorporating the believer into the events as if he were historically present. The difficulty of the problem is seen in the efforts made by his sympathetic critics to solve it. The Munich professor Söhngen tried to get over the difficulty by saying that Christ's acts being historical, they cannot be repeated or lifted out of their historical setting. He said the crucified Lord lives, exalted in heaven and bearing the marks of his passion – there is a supra-historical aspect to the Calvary event itself, that is the divine life of Christ who, by being sacramentally present, continues the saving event through time by being present. The presence of the saving events is personal, not historical. Obviously, Söhngen was trying to find a way round the inconsistency which Schillebeeckx later saw in Casel: that the mystery is enacted by the Lord who in his incarnation subjected himself to all the limitations of historical existence, yet we have events transported as no other historical events can be. Another critic, Warnach, tried his hand at overcoming the problem by reversing the idea – it is not the event which becomes present to man, but man who becomes present at the event. But the problem is not overcome. Recent writings like the Anglican-Roman Catholic eucharist agreement cite the principle of *anamnesis* (an act is 'present' in its effects) and that differs from Casel's notion of renewing the event itself.[2] As Schillebeeckx said, 'Whatever is historically past cannot now, in any way at all, be made once more actually present, not even by God himself, not even "in mystery"'.[3] We must acknowledge that, like the historical Christ, the saving acts have really died.

Mystery theology unifies Christ to the believer at the price of sacrificing time's integrity. Not all the resources of that system can loose the cross from the demands of time without devaluing the present eucharistic event, nor can it explain the eucharist as Christ's act without uprooting the cross from history. The problem is a recurring one – we have already seen Pius XII worried about a false mysticism in those who 'deceived by the glamour of what claims to be a higher mysticism, have the effrontery to say that we ought to cultivate the "pneumatic or glorified Christ", not the historical Christ'.[4] One way out of the problem of reconciling yesterday's cross with today's altar is to de-humanise Christ by removing historical constraints. Another way is to obliterate *today's* altar and remove man back through the ages – that was Warnach's way. A third way is to obliterate *yesterday's* cross – that was Casel's way. Sohngen's way of Christ's *personal* presence seems the most promising but it demands a fully human presence and that, as we shall see, was not a primary concern of mystery theology.

Mystery theology's constant difficulties over the boundaries of time appear again in the writing of Dom Anscar Vonier of Buckfast Abbey. His work, *A Key to the Doctrine of the Eucharist* was translated from the French in 1925 because, in reclaiming from Aquinas a doctrine of 'signification', he shed light on the problem. Sacraments are not arbitrary rites but must symbolise; effective signs they are, but signs for all that – they possess intrinsic meaning as well as extrinsic value. In a brilliant passage, Vonier says the past event of Christ's passion is the cause of that sanctification of which the present celebration is the essence and the future the goal. 'Every sacrament, then, announces something; it brings back the past, it is the voice of the present, it reveals the future.'[5] If a sacrament were to signify some non-historical thing, it would have no place in the chain of cause and effect; if it were a causative event only, it would have no place as a sign of a past event. A sacrament's efficacy depends upon its being a sign of the historical saving event. But even Vonier could not entirely get over the time problem. He was aware that Casel erroneously thought the sacrament evoked the presence of Christ's body and blood in their condition as at the crucifixion, that the immolated body of the Lord was present, not the glorified – thus violating Aquinas as well[6] – but Aquinas could assert the presence of the whole Christ, and therefore the glorified Christ, only by falling back on a doctrine of 'con-comittance', i.e. Christ is wholly present under each of the eucharistic species. This teaching, however, does not arise from consideration of the species and has to be imported from without.

Another problem is how to draw the boundaries between Christ and his Church. In holding to a mystery in which sacraments are nothing less than the acts of Christ himself, mystery theology was comfortable with the Pauline metaphor of Christ the Head of the Church, his mystical body. The temptation is to fall back on the Church as the mystical body and to push it for all it is worth. Pius XII sensed this danger also – in *Mystici Corporis* he attacked the sort of mysticism which muddied distinctions between Christ and the Church; he saw that the historical grounds of belief were at risk. Since the sacraments were understood generally to be the principal meeting place of Christ and his Church, it is vital that nothing in the liturgy be seen as adding to the confusion. Yet that is the sort of confusion the mystery theology engendered.

Weakness of the Parent System

The twofold difficulty of mystery theology – time and unbridled ecclesiasticism – stems from exclusive reliance on the powerful concept of the Church as Christ's mystical body – a reliance arising from the desire to uphold acts of the Church as being also historical acts of Christ. Nowhere is this reliance clearer than in *Mediator Dei* where the mystical – body metaphor is invoked thrice in the introduction, twice to explain that the Church perpetuates the priestly office of Christ, seven times to argue that worship must be interior as well as external, once each in the sections on hierarchy, the Divine Office, and non-liturgical devotions, and thrice to describe participation in the

19

eucharistic sacrifice. Only three times is the Church as the bride of Christ mentioned and these do not bear directly on the encyclical's argument. Casel had claimed the 'doctrine of the mysteries' was not one view among many but embodied the Church's official teaching – the truth of that claim comes across with a vengeance. Mystical body imagery centres our attention on Christ and his body the Church. It is a small step from there to an absorbing concern with the elements of which that body consists: Christ the Head, we the members, the body and blood of Christ, the eucharistic bread and wine, bread which ensures we are one body, the blood of Christ which gives the Church its spiritual life, water from the side of Christ, the washing of baptism – the *Anima Christi* shows the extent these concerns have penetrated the heart of Catholic spirituality. Mystery theology shares the same preoccupations as its parent sacramental theology, being essentially a species-centred system concerned with images of the body. The truth is that Casel had taken the parent theology just about as far as it could go, and no further.

> The fact is that the organic principle is not sufficient by itself to provide the generating impulse of an entire system. Catholicism – whether Roman, Orthodox, or Anglican – needs the polarizing influence of a different principle if it is to be prevented from running out on the one hand into a vague and ethereal mysticism, or on the other hand into a hard and rigid formalism.[7]

Too often have men suffered from a runaway organicism which treats the Church as if it were the kingdom of Heaven and all its attitudes and rules heavenly. Mystical-body teaching, unchecked, promotes a sort of ecclesiastical monophysitism in which human, sinful, and limiting characteristics are overpowered by the idea of being Christ's body. What on other considerations would be accounted arrogance is claimed to be the Church's due. Triumphalism waits in the wings. Analogously, species-centred theology encourages worshippers to be transfixed by the awesome majesty of what lies on the altar – human limitations are irrelevant. Bread and wine are destroyed in order that Christ's body and blood – the

20

divine body and blood in ordinary lay eyes – may be present. Popular sacramentalism presents a monophysitism which goes hand in hand with ecclesiastical pretensions.

The bitter Protestant-Roman Catholic eucharistic controversies show what happens when attention to the elements takes priority over the wider context of personal relations. Enthusiasts for transubstantiation were ready to draw and quarter consubstantiationalists despite the latter's devotion to Christ, and vice versa. Clearly, Christians with a 'low' doctrine of the elements could take communion with great reverence. Species-centred ideas achieve a proper and subordinate place in the context of God-man relationship understood in other terms. Five examples suffice. First, Protestant militants did Catholics grave injustice in considering the latter's devotion to the Blessed Sacrament to be mere gawking at a 'miracle of the altar', just as Catholics were mistaken in discounting the former's devotion as 'nude commemoration' merely because it did not stem from a 'high' species doctrine. Secondly, we note that there is no inevitable logical connection between receiving body and blood and a loving relationship with the living Christ.[8] Other considerations need to be invoked. Thirdly, the eucharistic elements do not by themselves relate anybody to anything – neither their existence nor their conversion into 'supernatural species' establishes a relationship, as the command 'take . . . eat . . . drink . . . in remembrance of me' shows. Response to the sacraments demands the obedient using, not mere possession, of them. Fourthly, the traditional sacramental system abandons its concern for the identity of converted elements entirely in its baptismal teaching. The fundamental sacrament of union with Christ has to be explained in non-species terms. Fifthly, Jesus's words at the Last Supper placed his references to his body and blood and by implication the eucharistic elements within a context of personal commitment and within the whole history of Israel – 'this is my body *given for you*, my blood *of the (new) covenant*'. The elements attain fulness of meaning in the setting of a covenant which is the purpose running through the whole biblical account from the creation narratives to the new Jerusalem and which gives its name to both old and new testaments.

Merely identifying the received elements does not account for a relationship between the recipient and his Lord. If the elements were totally unworldly, absolutely different from what we know in the world, we might see ourselves receiving a divine substance the effect of which is to transform us into divinity. But that is not what holy communion does. The Church has often used language about sharing in Christ's divinity, but only as a consequence of his sharing our humanity. What is true of the Incarnation is true of the sacraments. The sacraments relate us in the first instance to Christ's human nature. The most high-flown devotional language talks not of a divine substance but of body and blood – two more earthy terms it is hard to conceive. The teaching of John 6 is that we receive, not *manna*, but human attributes – body and blood. Aquinas, for all his emphasis on transformed elements, quotes Augustine in his seventh lesson for Corpus Christi to the effect that communion 'is with that general assembly and Church of God's holy children'[9] – the objects received are unmistakeably human and provide access to our fellow Christians. That communion with Christ's humanity is the objective of holy communion, as of all sacraments and all prayer, is clear from this remarkable passage of Louis Bouyer, writing in the late 1940s, and which is worth reading at length:-

To say the man who was Jesus has the very personality of the Son, of the Word of God, and that His finite humanity subsists in that infinite Person, means that that humanity does not distinguish itself, as personal, by all the intermediate limitations and reciprocal exclusions that distinguish our persons from one another. On the contrary, the humanity of Jesus is distinguished among all human individualities by its assumption into a transcendence which, because it overtops us, can also envelop us. Evidently the humanity of Jesus remains, in spite of this, no less finite, no less limited in all that composes it – body, soul, thought, feelings, volitions. But all that, in Him, does not subsist in its own individuality. Nothing there terminates in itself: all there is body, soul, mind, will, of an infinite one. And so, in opening His *human* individuality to the infinite instead of closing it and walling it in upon itself as our persons do with our individualities, the divine person of this man who is Jesus Christ enables it on the one hand to partake of all that belongs to man, and on the other hand confers upon it a supernatural power of communicating itself to every man.

Without doubt, in spite of everything – even of the fall itself, the unity of our species was so real that we remained relatively open to one another, and that this openness to all, even on a purely natural plane, remains the condition of the life of each one. But there are impassible barriers, for, independently of the fall, we are ourselves only in so far as we are not others. The closest bonds of friendship or affection do not permit us the least entry into the conscience of one another. This fundamental impossibility of a truly interior communication is a law only too familiar to the most ardent human lovers.

No such thing, on the contrary, between Christ and us; He can be close to us and we can become more intimate with Him than we are with ourselves. In the human nature which He shares with us through His birth from the Virgin Mary and which has become individual only by becoming His own, the Word has neither excluded nor particularized any human attribute. There is nothing in any of us – no thought, no feeling, no act – that He has not the power to make His own by the fact of His Incarnation. And, inversely, there is nothing in Him – no thought, no feeling, no act – that He has not the power to make ours. He, the just One, has borne all the weight of our sins; and we, the sinners, can possess His sanctity. His cross is our salvation. There is, however, this capital difference between Him and us: it is He who gathers us to Himself to recreate us, and not we who assimilate Him to ouselves. Thus, our sins have not made Him a sinner, but His sanctity will make us saints.

He is not one beside us, among us, between us; but He is above us all and embracing us all. Our persons in coming to His person are not added to nor fused with His: His person embraces all without blending them. It can then give everything to them and to each person as to all persons without losing anything thereby of that new humanity which is His – the humanity of the Word, of the Son, *Jesus*.[10]

For all its faithful reflection of the insipient monophysitism of its parent mystical-body system, mystery theology yearns for an encounter with Christ's humanity – a yearning which it has not the means to keep within reasonable bounds. Casel thought of the elements on the altar as the immolated Christ; here his yearning for the human Lord gets him into trouble. And Casel is not satisfied with uprooting elements from history – he talks of being present at the *actions* of Christ. Awareness of action in the liturgy – be it Christ's or ours – means attending to human characteristics which do not arise out of a species-dominated system. Dix once made a shrewd remark:

> I do not know that any thoroughgoing attempt has ever been made to state the truth along the lines of a theology of the eucharistic action instead of in terms of the metaphysical correlation of the elements with the Body and the Blood.[11]

But that is exactly what Casel wanted to do and could not do adequately given the limitations of the mystical-body, species-centred sacramental approach. It is ironic that a fellow Benedictine (albeit an Anglican one) was unaware of the attempt – Dix does not mention Casel in *The Shape of the Liturgy*; by 1959 Casel's work had not been collected in English.

Species-centred theology has dominated not only Roman Catholic teaching. The Anglican prayer book catechism defines a sacrament as 'an outward and visible sign of an inward and spiritual grace given unto us, ordained by Christ himself, as a means whereby we receive the same, and a pledge to assure us thereof'; we receive 'grace', and what is that if not unhuman? Grace sounds like a substance. Calvin moved away from species considerations and spoke of grace other than as a substance – a sacrament is a 'testimony of the grace of God towards us, confirmed by an outward sign, with a reciprocal attestation of our piety towards him'.[12] But John Wesley taught that sacraments were saving ordinances conveying grace, and access to humanity is almost forgotten. Cranmer followed Zwingli in holding that Christ is present in the eucharist (as elsewhere) by virtue of his divinity and that there is no participation in Christ's humanity by virtue of eucharistic elements. Where

Cranmer differed from Zwingli was in stressing that God, rather than the believer, makes use of the elements as instruments when they are used obediently.[13] Zwingli believed that participation in the body of Christ was irrelevant to Christian faith and anyway he denied that the holy can be mediated by sensible forms. For him, the eucharist was a picturesque way of stating (but not too picturesque, judging from his liturgy!) Christ's saving death and of fortifying faith in it – he admitted the latter point only after his debate with Luther. The eucharist was relegated to a lesser role than preaching and became an occasional ordinance, and *did not mediate humanity*. Both Luther, and Bucer (who corresponded with Cranmer and visited him in 1549), held participation in Christ's humanity to be possible but only Luther saw it coming through the elements – only Luther it seems held both that the eucharist gives access to Christ's humanity and that it does this through the elements received. Cranmer saw only baptism as affording participation in Christ's humanity (the major sacrament that has the least to do with species-centred thought, be it noted).

The tendency to deny or ignore access to Christ's humanity in the eucharist went hand in hand with liturgical practices. If early Christians received communion weekly (Acts 2:46), in some cases daily and even possibly reserved the sacrament at home for the purpose, the withholding of communion from the laity began early. Liturgy as a complicated, clerical affair, encouragement of awe-inspiring veneration for the consecrated elements, the loss of the Jewish liturgical heritage, increasing remoteness of liturgical language, the western development of low mass and fasting stipulations – all these deepened the isolation of the laity from communion. But access to the redeeming humanity is essential. What laypeople were denied in communion, they looked for in the tenderness of our Lady and the human characteristics of the saints or in non-liturgical devotions. Anglican equivalents to these gap-filling cults were Victorian sentimentality, reliance on the word of liturgy, matins and evensong which preached and read of an accessible Christ. Perhaps the churchmanship fights in Anglicanism can best be seen as the Evangelical attempt to approach Christ's humanity – they did a lot of talking about opening one's heart to Jesus – in the face of Catholic sacra-mentalism's concentration on divine attributes like authority, omnipotence and timelessness. For Rome, the post-Vatican II reforms built on the frequent-communion motif of Pius X and tried to restore attention to Christ's humanity both by biblical reading and by an analogous easing of contact in the liturgy between priest and people and between people and people. The Anglican parallel was sufficiently successful that Archbishop Ramsey feared the parish communion had degenerated into a form of 'togetherness'. May it be true that, in addition to exaggerated veneration of the elements fencing off the altar by intimidating the laity, lay communion was also paradoxically discouraged by so divinising the accessible Christ as to render his humanity unavailable – hence communion became irrelev-ant? To make love only occasionally, can be defended in the name of safeguarding its special importance, but some may suspect unrecognised need to be the real motive for abstention! 'Most sacred' comes to mean 'not necessary'.

Anglicans like Westcott took a different line from Cranmer even if they used Cranmer's liturgy – consider this comment on John 6 by Westcott:

> To eat is to take that into ourselves which we can assimilate as the support of life. The phrase 'to eat the flesh of Christ' expresses therefore, as perhaps no other language could express, the great truth that Christians are made partakers of the human nature of their Lord, which is united in one person to the divine nature; that he imparts to us now, and that we can receive into our manhood, something of his manhood, which may be the seed, so to speak, of the glorified bodies in which we shall hereafter behold him. Faith, if I may so express it, in its more general sense, leaves us outside Christ trusting in him; but the crowning act of faith incor-porates us in Christ.[14]

Gore makes much the same point:

> He [Jesus] plainly means them to understand that, in some sense, his manhood is to be imparted to those who believe in Him, and fed upon as a principle of new and eternal life. . . .It is the humanity of nothing less than the divine person which is to be. . .communicated to us.[15]

The writings of Bouyer, Westcott, and Gore, as well as mystery theology itself, disclose a yearning for access to Christ's humanity which neither mystery theology nor its parent sacramental system envisaged, encouraged or answered.

The Liturgy and Biblical Theology

The Liturgical Movement welcomed insights from 'biblical theology', an emphasis upon biblical teaching which complemented the vernacular's use and the exposition of the bible in preaching. In the meeting of biblical theology and liturgical renewal certain principles stood out.[16] First, the bible was to be the touchstone of all Christian liturgy. Scripture was not called on to provide detailed rubrics for the conduct of services but worship was to be faithful to bible teaching. The bible was seen, not as a collection of inspired propositions about God, but as the record of a people's historical response to God. On biblical grounds, the old opposition between the eucharist as a sacrifice and as a meal was laid low. Ever since Aquinas the Roman Catholic view had been that the separation between the consecrations of bread and wine was the sign of the sacrifice because it signified the separation of Christ's body and blood from each other on the cross. Louis Bouyer saw that consecration is not a self-contained action – consecration implies the consuming of the consecrated species. 'The Eucharist makes of Christ's sacrifice our own for the reason that He is there presented under the species of our food.'[17] Secondly (and especially important for the Roman Catholic Church), the liturgy was recognised as the best occasion for training the laity to know the bible. Both the Old and New Testaments were important to Christians. But beyond reading parts of the Old Testament in the services, that part of the bible made little contribution to the movement's liturgical rationale – only in later years, for example, was the notion of *anamnesis* recovered from both Old and New Testament sources to make sense of memorial in the eucharist.[18] Thirdly, the false dichotomy between word and sacrament was eroded. They were seen as complementary – each supported and depended on the other. One fruit of this new perspective was widespread adoption of the eucharist as the primary Sunday service, not only amongst Evangelical

Anglicans but also in the Methodist and Reformed churches. If the failure to build a truly balanced biblical rationale for eucharistic worship ill-served ecumenism, the use of common biblical and liturgical texts brought the churches' worship closer together.

Perspective on the Church in the World

Recalling the temptations of the 'parent system' to unbridled ecclesiasticism, we can see that liturgical renewal has not understood with precision the meaning of 'the world' and, consequently, the Church's role. A feeling of unease has long existed over the liturgy-revealed attitudes. The 1928 prayer book deleted the embarrassing qualification '*Christian* kings and rulers' in its long communion intercession and added prayers for missionaries and places of education – all part of the attempt to come to terms with the changed world 'outside' (as it remained natural to say). It seemed the Church had begun to take to heart the realities of the world. If *The Parish Communion* had 'but two references to evangelism'[19], the 1962 report of Parish and People, *The Parish Communion To-day*, a book only half the size, devoted an entire chapter to the 'Mission of the People of God'. Prayer is encouraged to back up missionaries in going 'out' into the world, the Church's task of proclamation is reduced to the reminder that each parish or rural deanery should send out a missionary. The world is to be 'transformed' in a kind of parallel to eucharistic consecration before it can be said to belong to God – shades of the old mystical-body monophysitism? We are exhorted to go out of liturgy into mission, to leave the sanctuary and go out 'into the bent and bungled world', presumably to put it right. 'Liturgy does not end at an ecclesiastical altar', we are told.

The model of the Church as a sanctuary from which the faithful descend from time to time to bear Christ into a godless world is unchallenged, despite the urgings to undertake 'relevant' mission which spring from the malaise over the gap between the Church's views and the reasoning of the world. Again and again we hear the command 'Go forth into the world', couched in archaic language which suggests it has biblical if not dominical authority. It first appeared in the

28

confused 1928 confirmation rite: 'Go forth into the world in peace; be of good courage. . .' Worshippers are to be propelled out of the church service with the dynamic sense of a mission to accomplish. They are, like the Norman invaders of England, given a special blessing over and above the sacrament, to help them in the desert, as interpreted here by a Presbyterian admirer of such blessings:

> With regard to the Dismissal and Benediction, it may be said that the former is of value in so far as a challenge to service of Christ in the world is presented to the people. This is followed by the Benediction, for they must never be dismissed and sent forth in their own strength, but 'in the name of the Lord',having God's blessing upon them.[20]

Apparently holy communion is an insufficient blessing! In the light of what was said about not being seen to uphold a relationship to Chirst's humanity, is it surprising?

The words 'go forth' sing various tunes in the bible:-

Old Testament

9 times:	does not apply to humans at all, e.g. predicated of righteousness or the Law spreading from Jerusalem, of locusts and wild asses, of evil and a lying devil, of a measuring rod used in new territory.
9 times:	inconsequential meanings, e.g. leaving a place like the ark, going to pick up one who is arriving, relieving oneself in the night, reconnoitring to discover leprosy or to count the dead after a battle.
7 times:	used negatively, e.g. unable to leave prison, being told not to leave, or not to be in any hurry.
5 times:	uninspiring meanings, e.g. to escape destruction, to surrender, being thrown out, ceasing to be a nuisance, exiled from the sight of God.
15 times:	warlike meanings, e.g. to set out to destroy, torment or enslave.
2 times:	to be joyful and to make merry.

	New Testament
Once:	to travel (Acts 16:3).
Once:	predicated of destroying devils (Rev.16:14).
Once:	used negatively, e.g. do not go forth (Matt.24: 26).
Once:	to go out to suffer and bear abuse with Jesus (Heb.13:13).

In the Pentecost passage of Acts 2, where we might expect to find the term at its most forceful, we find not a word about the apostles going forth into the world from outside it. Nor do early liturgies show concern with going forth 'into the world'. In the middle of the service, the deacon used to shout 'Depart, you catechumens, depart' (i.e. 'Get out!') and at the end the remaining worshippers were told to go. When we recall that early Christians met in the roomiest house available, belonging to an affluent layman, it was no doubt tactful for someone other than the host to say 'Now go home' – apart from the problem of people who always stay too long, it was dangerous to hang about!

If the world is not for worship, just where do we think the liturgy takes place? Does not the liturgy occur in the world and are not the worshippers every bit as much in the world when they are in church as they are in the bath? Mystical-body, sacramental theology swallows too eagerly the description 'in the world but not of the world' (It is encouraging that, unlike Series 2, the Series 3 revision omitted 'into the world' but the appearance of the Series 2 form as an alternative in the Alternative Service Book makes one wonder if the authors had yet seen the point). The liturgy is where the world draws most of its ideas about what the Church really thinks and it is where the faithful imbibe their perspective on the relation of the Church to the world. Since the sacraments are the heart of public worship, in sacramental teaching and in such pretentious posturing as we have just seen, the Church's role in the economy of salvation is at stake and along with it the relationship to the rest of creation. The 'parent system' does little to check a kind of ecclesiastical imperialism which sees the world as at worst a place to be subjugated or at best a place where Christ has to be taken, not a Galilee where he is waiting. The first idea is pretentious, the second irreverent. Springing from the

Church's current understanding of herself, liturgical reform has been unable to speak realistically of the world which is its setting.

The Liturgical Movement saw its task as fivefold. First, the liturgy had a pastoral ministry to be carried out in binding men closer to each other and to the Church as dispenser of grace. In encouraging intelligible language and rationalising liturgical structure, the movement made an impact on all liturgical worship. That is true even if modern language may have 'lost something – just how much is still a lively topic of debate. Secondly, the liturgy was to be brought under the chastening discipline of biblical doctrine. We have seen how this was inadequately done. Thirdly, the liturgy was to enable participation in the paschal mystery of Christ – revision of the latin Holy Week rites in 1950 shows this aim clearly. But we have seen that what is needed is a good deal more than mystical-body theology and species-centred sacramentalism can do. Fourthly, the liturgy was on all sides heralded as 'corporate'. Participation was the key word. But if membership of the body corporate is defined by baptism, a truly corporate worship was not achieved insofar as the baptismal community differed from the eucharistic community. Fifthly, the liturgy was seen as a tool of renewal. The extent to which that is possible depends on how well the sacramental system can be reconstructed on truly biblical lines to allow an integrated community to participate in the humanity of Christ, 'in the world' as well as in church.

Covenant and the Passion

If traditional sacramental theology reflects the character of its parent, mystical-body, doctrine of the Church, an alternative view of the sacraments will reflect an alternative doctrine of the Church. If such a doctrine of Church and worship is biblical, doing justice to the bible as a consistent entity, it will not just pick out useful bits; if it is biblical, it will be ecumenical, commending itself to Christians widely; it will compensate for the weakness of the system it corrects, making sense of historicity and marking out precisely the Church's boundaries and claims; it will provide access to Christ's humanity and show that such access is essential to our humanity; it will see the world as it is, not constructing a fantastic picture of the world as an alien land bearing no trace of its creator; it will demand a humble if vital task for the Church and sacraments and will encourage a proper Christian posture toward that created realm of which it is part.

Is there a doctrine which meets these criteria? Yes, there is; and it is based on the covenant. So prolonged and widespread has been the distortion of covenant teaching in some circles that the reader may lift up his hands in a gesture of disbelief. Since its enjoyment among the post-Calvinists in a spate of popularity during which time the covenant idea was wrenched hither and thither, reduced to the role of a propaganda tool, misunderstood, misapplied and trivialised to serve the interests of Christian internecine warfare, it has been paid only sporadic and superficial attention and, for the most part, ignored. So extensive was the disservice done to the Church by the covenant's self-styled champions that the rest of the Church dropped the notion. Left it alone, that is, until re-examination in the latter part of this century provided the means for a fresh and bracing reappraisal.

No Roman Catholic writer of the Liturgical Movement made anything of the covenant – the Church's mystical-body metaphor was enough for them. Cabrol's lengthy encyclopedia on worship contains no article on covenant, the early writers (Beauduin, Herwegen, Casel, Vonier, Laporta, and Guardini) ignored it as did later ones (Michonneau, Davis, the priests of St Séverin and St Joseph, and Jungmann). The covenant had no important place in their schemes of thought – even the *Catholic Encyclopaedia* barely mentions it in an article on symbolism and in one or two other places. *Mediator Dei*, that 'charter of the Liturgical Movement' (as Beauduin called it), does not even mention it. Protestants used the word more often but, as we shall see, most of them did not understand it. The covenant really begins with the idea that

> The faith of the Old Israel was created by a series of divine acts, beginning with the deliverance from the Egyptian bondage and culminating in the covenant on Mount Sinai. From the day that the agreement was ratified by the sprinkling of the blood of the sacrificial victim upon the altar and upon the people (Exod.24:7 & 8), the Israelites became a 'peculiar treasure' unto God, a chosen and precious possession, 'a kingdom of priests, and an holy nation.' [Exod.19:5 & 6].[1]

A covenant relationship with God was fundamental to Israel's self-awareness as a people from earliest times. The Old Testament scholar von Rad saw in the covenant kinship with Hittite treaties which were part of Israel's life even before the Exile.[2] Various strands in the Old Testament traditions had been woven together during the book's development to make a consistent account. First came the 'Covenant with the Patriarchs', brought into being by God; emphasis on response by Abraham and his successors is secondary to God's initiative. Second is the Sinai tradition which understood covenant as a one-way protective relationship established by God. Third is the J literary strand combining the two prior accounts and laying out the basic lines of the familiar Pentateuch. Fourth is the E or priestly tradition of the eighth century B.C. emphasising man's necessary response of obedience to God's initiative. The fifth and definitive formulation is the JE (or D) redaction of the seventh century B.C. which was expanded to take in Joshua, proclaiming a covenant resting on unique events in the history of the people: the promise of a new land made to Abraham before the servitude in Egypt (ca. 2100 B.C.), then the post-Egypt fulfilment of that promise in Joshua's time perhaps six centuries later. Without dwelling on Joshua or the expansion of the covenant people from a small group fleeing Egypt into the whole of Israel or the introduction of a universal dimension to covenant, by the P redaction's introduction of Noah in the sixth or fifth centuries B.C., it suffices to point out that by ca. 850 B.C. (the date of the J document) this oral tradition was written down and that from at least that time, and probably much earlier, the covenant was regarded as the definitive principle for the identity of Israel.

The early Christian Church saw its Lord as the covenant's true fulfilment, and herself as the people of the New Covenant. What Jeremiah 31:31–34 and Hebrews 8:7–13 had anticipated was fulfilled in Christ. The early Christians saw themselves as the heirs to the Jewish hope, 'as Abraham's seed, heirs according to promise' (Galatians 3:29). As the covenant's true heirs, they took over the Jewish scriptures and Israel's titles. 'The New Covenant was ratified by the cross and the sequel through the resurrection and the subsequent mission of the Spirit was the founding of the New Israel.'[3] The Epistle to the Hebrews makes much of the parallel between Moses as the mediator of the old covenant and Jesus, the mediator of the new covenant. In each case, the covenant was established with blood: 'For when, as the Law directed, Moses had recited all the commandments to the people, he took the blood of the calves . . . and sprinkled the law-book itself and all the people, saying, 'This is the blood of the covenant which God has enjoined upon you'. . . . Indeed, according to the Law, it might almost be said, everything is cleansed by blood and without the shedding of blood there is no forgiveness.' (9:19–22). But the old covenant had to be made new, '(God) has pronounced the first one old' (8:13). A new covenant far better than the old has come into being (8:6); we see 'Jesus the mediator of a new covenant, whose sprinkled blood has better things to tell' (12:24).

The covenant is, first and foremost, an unconditional gift from God and is brought into being by his own initiative, springing out of his total commitment to man's redemption. The Protestant theologian Vriezen, put it strongly:

34

The Covenant may, indeed, be broken by Israel, and in that case God punishes His headstrong and wilful people, but that does not mean that the Covenant, the circle, is broken by God. Even if God rejects the empirical Israel in its entirety for some time, that does not mean that Israel is rejected altogether. None of the prophets thought that the judgment of the people of their days implied the destruction of the people as such![4]

The second truth about the biblical covenant proceeds from the first – the story is a continuous saga of grace. There is no fundamental division between Old and New Testament covenants. In the earliest Old Testament tradition itself, God calls his people into a relationship with him which is not their's 'by nature' and the terms of which are not settled by them.[5] If Calvin knew perfectly well that the Jews 'were parties to the Gospel covenant'[6] and saw the Old Testament Law as a schoolmaster leading to Christ and neither temporary nor evil, it is obvious those who claimed to be his followers did not. In the Second Scots Confession of 1580 we see what could be done with Calvin: the dialectic between Law and Gospel has been obliterated. In 1648 the Westminster Confession went further and called the old a 'covenant of works', a contract dependent on the fulfilment of conditions – the new covenant was an irresistible compulsion which has not even the virtue of a contract; the latter they called the 'covenant of grace'. This line persisted in Reformed teaching up to this century as we see in the Westminster Bible Dictionary (1880) which dubs the old covenant a covenant of works and reduces it to Adam with nary a mention of Abraham, Moses, Noah, or Jeremiah. The false dichotomy turns up elsewhere too, as when the Roman Catholic pastor Pius Parsch wrote 'the old covenant, based on Law, was sealed with the blood of an animal victim: the new covenant of Grace is sealed with the Blood of Christ'.[7]

This lopsided hydra grew out of an uncritical acceptance of St Paul's words in Galatians which ignored his teaching elsewhere on the covenant. Paul contrasted Abraham's covenant ('a proleptic realization of the covenant in Christ' and hence a covenant of faith) with the Sinai covenant which he saw as one of Law whose purpose was to make men aware of their sin so that they would welcome the new covenant of forgiveness.[8] Christian polemics took on an anti-Jewish bias once it became clear that Israel as a whole had rejected Jesus. It seemed natural to dwell on Jeremiah's prophecy, 'Behold, the days come . . . that I will make a new covenant . . . not according to the covenant I made with their fathers' (31:31 & 32). Paul's treatment of covenant in Galatians is understandable but the passages on which his Sarah-Hagar analogy is based (Gen 16:15 and 21:3 & 9) will not bear the weight he put upon them – there is even a covenant of sorts made with Ishmael, the bondmaid's son and it is not slavery. It is a promise in response to Abraham's grief over the prospect of Ishmael's being slighted and it amounts to a promise that Ishmael's descendants will also be a nation (Gen 21:13). Furthermore the quotation from the prophet, 'Rejoice, thou barren that bearest not . . . for the desolate hath many more children than she which hath an husband' (Isaiah 54:1 quoted in Gal 4:27) is more apt when applied to the bondmaid than Abraham's wife! In Galatians, Paul forgets to mention Moses, the key figure of the Sinai covenant! We have only to look at Paul's mention of Moses elsewhere to see his view of Sinai. In 1 Corinthians 10:2–5, Paul draws a parallel between the pillar of cloud and baptism and an inept parallel between manna and drink in the desert and the eucharist and says that all drew their food from Christ. But no dichotomy appears, even in that passage.

Paul also turned his attention to Moses in 2 Cor 3:6–18 where Moses's face shines with brightness, reflecting God's glory as he brings down the covenant from Sinai. In Exodus 34:29–35 from which Paul draws his reference, Moses wore a veil so as not to frighten the people, so luminous did his covenant role make him, while for Paul Moses wears a veil to *disguise* the fading brightness of his face and spare them the depressing truth about the covenant's flaws. Since Paul has no interest in likening Moses and Jesus as mediators of covenant, he invents a tortured polemical exegesis to minimise the former. For all that, Paul still showed traces of reverence for Moses's covenant – in 2 Timothy 3:8 & 9 he states his conviction that his opponents are like Jannes and Jambres, 'men of corrupt mind and counterfeit truth' who opposed Moses, and they will suffer the same fate as did Moses's opponents.

The Vatican II documents reveal a reappraisal – the old covenant is a fore-shadowing of the Church[9], that it is a complementary covenant to the new is found in the writings of Augustine, Cyril of Jerusalem, Irenaeus, and Theodore of Mopsuestia.

God, the inspirer and author of both testaments, wisely arranged that the new testament be hidden in the Old and the Old be made manifest in the New. For, though Christ established the new covenant in his blood . . . , still the books of the old testament with all their parts, caught up into the proclamation of the gospel, acquire and show forth their full meaning in the new testament and in turn shed light on it and explain it.[10]

There is even a hint that the covenant furnishes the ground for a doctrine of worship – 'The renewal in the eucharist of the covenant between the Lord and man draws the faithful into the compelling (perhaps an unfortunate word to use, given the history of covenant doctrine) love of Christ and sets them on fire.'[11]

Our description of the Church as the covenant people answers the demands of the criteria set out above for a corrective to mystical-body doctrine. First, it draws on the whole bible – Old and New Testaments – and shows a recurring theme which gives cohesion to the whole drama, from creation to redemption, bestowing its very name on the scriptures.

Secondly, building on recent Protestant scholarship and the decisions of Vatican II, it provides a rationale which can be understood by various Christian traditions. It also has for Hebrew religion and culture a sympathy not found in the mystical-body teaching.

Thirdly, it escapes the entanglements of the alternative system. Past and present are no problem in their being separated and their integrity is not under fire. We do not have to get out of a now-and-then dilemma since we never get into one. Christ who died once is the mediator of the new covenant brought about by his death, ratified by his rising, made contemporary by his eternal heavenly intercession, and is entered into at baptism and renewed in eucharist. Since the covenant is built on promise, the future is a present reality without compromising its nature as future. Tension between present, past and future is natural to the covenant and without it there could be no covenant. Contrasted to mystical-body theology's runaway organicism, the covenant applies humbling limits to the Church's claims. Behind these limits lie a sharp distinction between Christ and his Church and between the Church and the Kingdom of God. The world was not created to become the Church, but the kingdom of God.

Fourthly, the covenant knows no way to God except through humanity. The mediator of covenant, indispensable to its creation, is fully human – Moses was mediator of the old covenant as Jesus is mediator of the new. The words of Jesus at the Last Supper assert his humanity to be the objective and the means for the creation and maintenance of his covenant – 'this cup is the (new) covenant in my blood'. As we shall presently see, covenant relationships enhance human characteristics instead of doing them down.

Fifthly, the world is seen with fresh insight since it is the place where the covenant is lived out. It is no alien territory – it is marked by certain paschal signs as the place of Christ's presence, signs which enable the Church to detect the world as the stage for divine action.

Sixthly, the covenant approach provides a powerful rationale for the sacraments since entry to the covenant and its renewal in both Old and New Testaments occur through signs which encourage Christians to assume a realistic attitude toward the world they inhabit.

Divine Initiative and Commitment

The bible teaches that God cannot be found. He is known only when he chooses to be known. In a sustaining environment, man saw the hand of one with a purpose for his creatures and one who cared for them even when they disobeyed. Apart from God's choice, Adam would have heard no voice in the garden 'in the cool of the day', Isaac no command to sacrifice nor to hold his hand, Noah no saving word, the Patriarchs no promise, Moses would have had no covenant to reveal, Jesus would have heard no baptismal voice. In the first instance, God spoke to individuals and not to categories or classes: Adam, Isaac, Noah, Moses, Mary. Once revealed, the knowledge that God had spoken spread to communities growing from the key individuals – Adam and his wife and children, Isaac and his myriad descendants, Noah and his relatives and then the whole of mankind, Moses and the people, Mary and her family and later the disciples to whom they were closely related. The unique relationship between the Father and Jesus is spread abroad – the sole remnant of the old covenant gathers round him the re-constituted kingdom of David.

The scandal of particularity – a scandal believed by some to consist in the favouring of some persons and not others by God – is necessitated by the need to touch humanity not just in its flesh and blood but also in the inner depths where each man is alone and unique. Particularity is the corollary of personality. The needs of one person are unique and governed by unique factors – *Abraham* had one son and no prospect of another heir, *Abraham* was wracked by the command to sacrifice and to spare, the ram caught in the thicket spoke directly to *Abraham's* condition. God met each person in the lonely place where no one else stood. In Jesus this truth is paramount – that unity which Christians share is possible because of the acknowledged uniqueness of Jesus.

Though each meeting of soul with soul is unique, it requires the presence of others to mirror it. No one deeply knows or loves another in a social vacuum. Lovers may regret others' presence, but others are essential in coming to know the personality of the one who is loved! Failure to recognise this appears in our arrogant exaltation of romantic love – an individualistic cult which discounts social context – over arranged marriage despite the rate of break-down in the former type. Certainly, the reactions to Jesus revealed his person, but more than that is meant. In their changing personalities those around Jesus are like icons in whose faces we see Christ. The accessible humanity of Christ (in Bouyer's phrase) has touched them in their individuality – they become mediators of Jesus who is open to them and to whom they become open. Mary 'ponders these things in her heart', tells the wedding party to obey Jesus and takes John the beloved disciple as her son; Peter, the blunt and impetuous fisherman, becomes the Rock; Mary Magdalen turns from exploitation of her body to caring for Jesus's body in the tomb; even Judas Iscariot becomes an icon as one who, retreating into his own desires, betrays a Jesus who would not be a 'success' and fulfil expectations. The poor, the sick, those in prison who are mediators of Jesus (as in Matthew 25) are not so as classes but as persons.

The poignancy of relationships between Jesus and those around him seems almost bigger than life. Mary Magdalene bathes his feet with her tears, wipes them with her hair, covers his feet with kisses and pours precious ointment over him – gestures – so extravagant that Judas protests. John the beloved disciple leans against Jesus, Peter weeps, those formerly possessed leap with joy at their deliverance. And why has so much been made, as in St John's Gospel, of the relationship between Jesus and his mother, extracting the intimacy of that relationship out of its setting and commending it to the very prayers of the faithful as a relationship for us to enter into, or why so much emphasis on the commendation of Mary and John to each other as mother and son? Of course Mary would need to be looked after, but did John need a mother? The real reason is neither 'idolatry' (though that could develop) nor recognition of an abstract 'communion of saints' doctrine, but is simply the need to proclaim the eternal depth of human love that Jesus brought about in those he touched. In the cult of the saints, the Church sets forth a communion first and foremost between each saint and Jesus, the most truly human of all.

The ability to respond to God's initiative comes by grace and also is mediated. Christian teaching is that the Holy Spirit sanctifies. This happens however, not by a descent which ignores human relationships. The Spirit is mediated by those in whom Christ dwells and touches their humanity so that they can respond to the love poured forth. The covenant is made with someone enabled to respond by the faithfulness of those about him. Baptism, for example, both imparts the Spirit to an individual and in forgiving him places him within a forgiven community of human icons reflecting the presence of Christ in their forgiving humanity. The eucharist feeds the person who perceives others responding to Christ – others who are loved by Christ and by himself. Likewise, the covenant is known by an individual who perceives a witness to that covenant in other individuals. While covenant safeguards an individual's humanity, covenant is made in community. Unlike some forms of social organization, the covenant community enhances each member's personhood. God's initiative and commitment are demonstrated, not only by keeping up the covenant he has instituted but also by the nature of the community it upholds – this is the sort of community we would expect, considering it was based on the covenant which Jesus brought about by his death 'for us'.

Human personality is manifested not only in the way an individual plays his unique part, but also in the revelation made by a particular human, Jesus Christ. Incarnation in that one person took place both in order to translate God 'into human terms' – as is commonly said – and also (what is not always recognised) to touch each man with the infinitely accessible humanity of one man, Jesus Christ. Even in the Old Testament, the covenant was not the handing over of a document by God but a face to face meeting. The personal nature of the covenant is revealed in Jesus Christ who is himself the covenant 'in blood'. In the new covenant, all the characteristics of the covenant remain and become unmistakeably personal. What distinguishes the Old and New Testament covenants from each other is not some imagined difference between works and grace but simply that in the New Testament the covenant has come from God in the full humanity of Jesus Christ. In both covenants, human mediation is the means by which the covenant becomes a blessing.

The dependability of the covenant is rooted in God's nature and that leads writers like Schillebeeckx to see even the act of creation as a covenant act, calling the creation 'the beginning of the covenant of grace'.[12] The primitive Christian hymn in 2 Timothy 2:11–13 sums up the dependability of God, 'If we are faithless, he keeps faith, For he cannot deny himself'. This confidence is rooted in the conviction that the word of God, once uttered, cannot be retracted – 'My covenant will I not break, nor alter the thing that is gone out of my lips' (Ps. 89:34). In the Old Testament the only 'covenant' 'broken' by God is one with the heathen whose punishing arm had been

41

previously stayed from striking rebellious Israel! (Zech.11:10). The 'Songs of the Servant of Yahweh', like the ancient Christian hymn, record the steadfastness, 'for the mountains may depart, the hills be shaken, but my love for you will never leave you and my covenant peace with you will never be shaken, says Yahweh who takes pity on you'.[13] The Lord who creates, redeems as well, and that too is a covenant act because it perpetuates the faithfulness of the Lord who will not allow what he has established to be thwarted by sin – 'What if some of them (the; Jews) were unfaithful? Will their faithlessness cancel the faithfulness of God? Certainly not!', Paul writes the Romans (3:3 & 4). The liturgy proclaims divine initiative and faithfulness as the beginning of the paschal mystery we know as creation.

The Experience of Loss

The experience of loss or the real threat of loss is a characteristic of the covenant both for the giver and the recipient. God's commitment to Noah (Gen.9:6) carried with it the risk of suffering rebuff, as any lover declaring himself knows very well is the risk he runs. Likewise, Noah's obedience meant that everyone else thought him to be mad (7:5, 7–9). God's self-limitation in promising not to repeat the flood (9:11) and his promise to look upon the rainbow and remember (9:6) also speak of loss. Both Abram and Sarai lost their familiar names (17:5, 15). Abraham lost his fore-skin if not considerable dignity (17:10). His obedience in preparing to sacrifice Isaac meant the loss of his one hope of true descendants (cap. 22). Others, outside the covenant, also suffer loss – Ishmael had to take second place to Isaac (17:20). Moses's reaction to the covenant moved him to fast in the Lord's presence (Exod.34:28), the people gave up their jewellery and gold (35:22) and submitted to circumcision (Deut.10:16). The new covenant required the humility of the Son before his Father, and before the people in suffering the death of a criminal. Jesus was overwhelmed with impending loss and stated that he would sup with his followers no more until he comes to his kingdom (Matt.26:29, Mk.14:25, Lk.22:18). We need only mention the lonely cry from the cross to see what loss was entailed for the mediator of the new covenant (Matt.27:46, Mk.15:34).

Ordinary covenant-like events disclose the same characteristic of deprivation. The bridegroom who feels a sense of loss upon entering the marriage covenant is a common butt for the lucky fellows who have as yet escaped. A political covenant of union between states entails loss of independence and the removal of customs barriers and passport controls. In sexual relations, the sense of loss is well known – we recall Shakespeare's word for orgasm, 'dying'.

The Experience of Gain

The sense of loss in covenant is, nonetheless, accompanied by the experience of gain. God's commitment to Noah meant the prospect of his will being implemented to fill the earth. Noah's obedience menat that he would have a future and descendants (Gen.17:2) – the beasts will regard them with fear and dread; Noah gains a feeling of security (8:11–17). Abraham is told he will father many generations (17:2) and kings (17:6) and that a promised land awaits (17:8), that he will have a legitimate son (17:5). In the moment of his greatest loss, the ram caught in the thicket meant reprieve and the demonstration that God had provided the matter of sacrifice. Others, outside the covenant, sense gain too – Ishmael will also be a nation. The skin of Moses's face shone (Exod.34:30) and such was the elation that the chief men of Israel 'beheld God, and ate and drank' (24:11). While they gave up their riches, they gained a tabernacle to be with them (35:10), they were promised wealth (Deut.8:18) and the knowledge of being a people for God's own possession to be set high above all nations (26:18, 19).

Some see this as an insult to divine sovereignty. For example, in a book about *substitution* (the idea that man's reconciliation to God was effected by Christ standing in our stead to suffer the consequences of sin), Van Buren notices a strange weakness in Calvin's logic. Calvin sees God having certain characteristics or attributes which are hidden from man in Christ, even though Christ has come to *reveal* God. For example, Christ does not reveal God's glory, which presumably he means in the sense of triumph:

The divine nature was in a state of repose, and did not exert itself at all whenever it was necessary, in discharging the

43

office of Mediator, that the human nature should act separately according to its peculiar character;[14]

The separation of the two natures, however, makes it hard to see the Incarnation's implications. It is true that Calvin was echoing the teaching of Leo who attacked the teaching of Eutyches in A.D. 449 that after the Incarnation the distinction between the divine and human natures of Christ no longer existed. But in saying 'each nature keeps its own characteristics without diminution, and as the form of God does not annul the form of a servant, so the form of a servant does not impair the form of God' (Letter of Leo to Flavian), Leo maintained the different characteristics in such a way – at least it is clearly his intention – as not to negate any of the characteristics. 'Thus,' writes Leo, 'the properties of each nature and essence were preserved entire, and went together to form one person; and so humility was taken up by majesty, weakness by strength, mortality by eternity; and for the purpose of paying the debts which we had incurred, the nature that is inviolable was united to the nature that can suffer.' We can see what Leo had in mind if we ask what God's glory revealed in Christ consisted of. Was it not the 'form of a servant', the humility of Christ, showing the unbounded love of God, which constitutes the revelation of God's glory? Calvin seems to have thought of a glory which cannot but be muted by humility. But the kind of glory revealed both by the condescension in becoming incarnate and in his obedience to his Father is the only kind of glory we can strive for or even emulate. Far from concealing glory, it reveals it in the only way we can comprehend. Without that sort of glory, God's glory is not revealed to man. The early Christians did not think Christ had thwarted the promise of Isaiah, 'the glory of the Lord shall be revealed, and all flesh shall see it together.' (40:5). The fourth evangelist speaks what the Church believed had happened, 'And the word was made flesh and dwelt among us, (and we beheld his glory, the glory of the only begotten of the Father) full of grace and truth.' (1:14).

Calvin thought God had held back his glory in the Incarnation rather than putting glory into human terms. If the divine nature was 'in a state of repose', how could Christ reveal God? If God was in Christ, that was because God alone could redeem man. In that activity, he manifests himself. Quite apart from how Calvin could possibly know God was holding something back – after all he believed we could only know what Christ had revealed – we are by Calvin involved in a system where reluctance by God to commit himself is apparent. Not only is the concurrent gain-through-loss negated, but the covenant principle that God has committed himself to man is lost sight of. Leo's view sustains the conviction that the personality of Christ itself acts in accordance with the covenant trait of the greater being active in the lower. Further, the action of God in the Incarnation shows a like concurrent gain-and-loss. Still further, in revealing his glory through the medium of humility, God provided a way for man's humility to achieve glory. The possibility of man's participation in Christ's humanity has therefore opened the path to man's deification through Christ's humanity. We have in Christ not a substitute for us, but the means of aspiring to obedience, and glory. The gain-through-loss does carry a threat to divine sovereignty, but it is no insult. It is the heart of the paschal mystery. For all Jesus's humiliation, he knows he is being glorified (Jn.17) – if he is lifted up on the cross, he will draw all men to himself (12:32). The Last Supper is celebrated in the knowledge of the new kingdom's inauguration. Even in near-despair, Jesus proclaims a victory – 'It is finished' (19:30, cf. 17:4).

The bridegroom may be losing his freedom but he does so for a greater gain, and his jocular mates know that full well. Political union between states is only entered upon for the sake of mutual advantage. And love is the mystery where gain is achieved through loss. Reason may fail to comprehend how such loss and gain are often not separated but concurrent, but our inablility to understand how it can be does not undo the reliability of our experience. What is more difficult to admit is that all givers as well as recipients, even God, suffer simultaneous loss and gain. That is one of the unavoidable consequences of taking human nature. The presence of death in life and the process of life through death is what the Church calls the paschal mystery.

In both old and new covenants there is a tension between the present and the future. We have already seen that this tension is not a problem to be got over but natural to covenant. Abraham knew God as promise, 'Here now is my covenant with you: you shall become the father of a multitude of nations' (Gen.17:4). Von Rad understood this attribute of the covenant as the constituent principle of Israel, 'It was only in her position in the minimum between a promise and its fulfilment that Israel understood herself as a unit'.[15] Tension between present and future in terms of promise exists for the new covenant too – the holy people has come into being, yet true holiness is to be achieved. With desire did Christ yearn to eat the passover with his disciples (Lk.22:15), but he will not drink of the fruit of the vine until the kingdom has come (Mk.14:25 etc.). The Church's unity is both a fact and a goal to be achieved. As with the experience of gain-through-loss, some Christians try to get out of the tension between the reality of a sinful Church and the promise of indestructibility by resorting to an idea of the true, invisible Church known only to God, set over against the visible Church which, it is implied, lacks authenticity and cannot claim to be the covenant community. But tension is maintained only if the true Church is here and now visible, yet awaiting the fulfilment of promise.

The covenant is neither a piece of paper nor just a promise present in the believer's mind. When Israel was led out of Egypt, Yahweh promised that he would be with them himself (Lev.26:11,12). J.G. Davies put it like this:

> they left the holy Mountain and began their march on Canaan, they believed that that promise was being kept and that their God was indeed at their head; henceforth He was present with them and talked with them [2 Sam.7:6, 7]. This Covenant-Presence was inseparable in the religious thought of Israel from their status as the Covenant People: 'where one is, there the other must be, not temporarily but for ever'.[16]

In the same way, the promise which Christ made at the Last Supper when he was present with his followers, brought into being a covenant that likewise required his presence.

The newly-married couple sees some promise for the future; if they did not see their marriage as a 'promising one', they would not undertake it. The fulfilment of that promise demands the presence of each. The sexual act may produce a child which, in its mother's womb, bears in a certain sense the presence of both parents. Any promise which is more than 'just so many words', carries in one sense or other, the presence of the giver and recipient. The epistle to the Hebrews tells the members of the new covenant that they stand before 'Mount Zion and the city of the living God . . . and God the judge of all . . . and Jesus the mediator of a new covenant' (12:22–24).

The Bias toward the Universal

In the covenants of Noah, Abraham and Moses, as of Jesus, movement is from the one to the many, from one man, tribe or nation to the universal. Unlike Babylon, Israel did not see her special position based on a mythology wherein the Israelites sprang up as the natural offspring of a tribal god. She was one of the nations and her identity was based on what she had learned in her history. What began with Adam stumbled in the fiasco of Babel, but the covenant of Noah was for all and it persisted – the beasts will fear Noah and his heirs; to restrict that to Jews would be meaningless. Abraham's covenant is promulgated as a blessing to 'all the families of the earth through Abraham'. The new covenant is for all mankind, as even mistaken and harmful pretensions to ecclesiastical imperialism testify.

Civilizations have been vulnerable to the temptation to turn inwards, turning their privileges into occasions for pride. Some have done so in blatant self-assertion, others smugly. Reinhold Niebuhr looked at *realpolitik* in 1941:

> In modern international life Great Britain with its too strong a sense of security, which prevented it from taking proper measures of defence in time, and Germany with its maniacal will-to-power, are perfect symbols of the different forms which pride takes among the established and the advancing social forces. The inner stability and external security of Great Britain have been of such long duration that she may

be said to have committed the sin of Babylon and declared, 'I shall be no widow and I shall never know sorrow.' Germany on the other hand suffered from an accentuated form of inferiority long before her defeat in the World War. Her boundless contemporary self-assertion, which literally transgresses all bounds previously known in religion, culture and law, is a very accentuated form of the power impulse which betrays a marked inner insecurity.[17]

Israel was not immune from that temptation. John the Baptist warned them 'do not presume to tell yourselves, "We have Abraham for our father", because, I tell you, God can raise children for Abraham from these stones.' (Matt.3:9). A universal bias in covenant is to be expected since all mankind is loved by the paschal Lord.

4

The Signs of Covenant

The manner of entry into the old covenant was, it was believed, established by God, the covenant's author. The means of entry was circumcision and was also of divine origin (Gen.17:11; Jer.4:4). And the Christians agreed: Paul regarded it as the seal of Abraham's faith (Rom.4:11) and the sign of the covenant under which Abraham was to become father to many nations (Rom.4:17 & 18). In the Church's eyes, the means of entry to the new covenant was also given by the covenant's author. 'Baptism is spiritual circumcision by means of which the individual is brought into the Covenant.'[1] it is the 'seal' till the day of redemption – the uses of the word 'seal' 'in connection with baptism, a Jewish term for circumcision indicate that the Fathers were making no innovation in emphasising the parallel.'[2] Paul wrote to the Colossians, 'In him also you were circumcised, not in a physical sense, but by being divested of the lower nature; this is Christ's way of circumcision' (2:11).

But the old covenant had to be renewed; each generation had to be brought into it afresh (Deut.5:3 *et seq.*). It was renewed at Shechem in the time of Joshua (Joshua 24:14–25), and at other times. At passover came the annual renewal in which the past deliverance by God was appropriated, as illustrated in the feast of Azymes, at the season's end, when the leader declares 'that the whole of Israel, past and present, and he himself, have all come out of the Egyptian bondage: "It is because of that which the Lord did for *me* when *I* came forth out of Egypt".'[3] Like the entry into the covenant at circumcision, the application of the covenant to each Jew at passover – applying incidentally, to both sexes – was by divine initiative and command and could therefore relate to the original act of god (Exod.13;9 & 10).

The new covenant, too, had to be renewed and applied to each man, not only because new men are born but because of the disruptive power of sin. 'The eucharist is the sacrificial meal by means of which the covenant-relationship is renewed.'[4] At the Last Supper the disciples were told of the meaning of the passion to follow; Christ explicitly spoke of the new covenant in his blood. That supper took place within a passover context, regardless of whether it was the passover or the day before. In other words, the eucharist of the new covenant was instituted against the background of the one Jewish feast specifically concerned with the renewal of covenant. In the Last Supper the emphasis was upon the renewal of Israel in a new covenant, while in the eucharist the emphasis is on renewal of the baptismal covenant itself. In the last Supper, a banquet charged with the meaning of passover, christ had proclaimed not only the meaning of his coming death but had also given the eucharist as the means whereby his covenant would in future be renewed in the members of that covenant.

Participation in the paschal mystery of Christ comes through participation in the new covenant. Since entry to the covenant and its renewal are by the signs given by the covenant's author and proclaimed by its mediator, those signs share naturally the covenant's characteristics. Baptism proclaims God's total commitment in an act of his choosing, the eucharist does the same. Baptism signifies the experience of loss by drowning, the eucharist signifies the death on the cross. Baptism signifies the experience of gain by forgiveness and entry into eternal life, the eucharist proclaims forgiveness and is the 'medicine of immortality'. Baptism signifies the promise of life in the kingdom to come as well as giving membership in the Church, eucharist provides the heavenly banquet's foretaste as it provides a feast on the Lord's sacramental body and blood. Baptism invites all; the eucharist, reminiscent of the parable of the Great Supper, proclaims the death of Christ for all, and calls them to faith. Paul concluded that in celebrating eucharist we show forth the Lord's death till he comes – he summarises the correspondence between the signs and the covenant:

Initiative:	the *Lord's* death, till *he comes*.
Loss:	the Lord's *death*.
Gain:	till he *comes*.

Promise:	*till* he comes.
Universal bias:	*show forth the Lord's* death.
	(1 Cor.11:26).

Particularity

The particular signs of the covenant provide the means of membership, enable the members to renew their membership, set forth the nature of the covenant, and bear witness to the character and will of the covenant's author. As the signs to which Christ's promise of perpetual companionship and the hope of salvation are attached, they are indispensable to the covenant's fulfilment. As the eighteenth century Archdeacon of Middlesex, Daniel Waterland, put it:

> In short, Sacraments are transactions of two parties, wherein God bears a share as well as man, and where the visible signs have an inseparable conjunction with the invisible graces signified, when duly administered to persons worthy. *Verbal professions, singly considered, come far short of what has been mentioned, and therefore cannot be presumed to amount to a renewal of the covenant, like the other.*[5]

Ironically, not all those who made the most of covenant saw the point. Calvin saw the signs as ratifying what had already taken place. Wesley thought covenant renewal a scriptural idea and had been reared in the Laudian notion that those who broke their part of the covenant had to renew it in holy communion. But later Methodist renewal rites purposely avoided Easter to avoid conflicting with the eucharist at the parish church and, after Wesley's death, completely disconnected it from the eucharist. The 1857 United Methodist Free Churches' service book pathetically provided for the Lord's Supper at the covenant renewal service 'if time permit'.[6] Though the 1936 book linked covenant renewal and the sacrament, it provided the latter as a distinct rite to be held after the former. The willingness to detach covenant renewal from its sign was just that sort of verbal profession Waterland had talked about.

As well as the use of particular signs rather than others, we have to consider the knotty problem of particular persons being chosen, authorised or ordained to act for the covenant

51

community. the issue of eucharistic presidency stands out. It arises in a scheme like the Ten Propositions of 1980–81 which envisages churches entering into inter-communion despite an initial period when not all eucharistic presidents will be priests in the episcopal succession. Such eucharists will be celebrated, however, by churches not individuals, and moreover, by churches committing themselves to unity in response to their common baptism, and agreeing the form of ministry and episcopal transmission they will observe henceforth for authorising presidents of the eucharist. Their response of unity on the basis of baptism amounts to a determination to renew the covenant, and that is what the eucharist is for.

The covenant sheds more light on the role of presiding individuals. The individual in the covenant – Abraham, Noah, Moses, Jesus – acts for the many in that what begins with one person springs into a community; the controlling persons in covenant are servants of the community. The priests and Levites were appointed to serve and none was to usurp their role. The same servant characteristic appears in the new covenant, but there is an all-important difference. Moses was told by God that his people would be 'a kingdom pf priests, a consecrated nation' (Exod.19:5) but in taking up this note for itself, the Church saw the place of priesthood within the covenant to be radically different. As Hebrews is at pains to point out, the old covenant priests offer sacrifices again and again, for their sacrifices 'can never bring the worshippers to perfection for all time' (10:1, *cf.* v. 11) whereas 'Christ offered for all time one sacrifice for sins' (10:12), 'for by one offering he has perfected for all time' the members of the covenant (10:14). What Moses the mediator of the old covenant could never do, Jesus the mediator of the new covenant has done. The need to repeat that sacrifice would imply its insufficiency and, in saying that it need not be repeated (quite apart from whether it *can* be repeated), we see that the true priesthood in the new covenant is in Jesus Christ himself. What the old covenant saw as a nation of priests demanded a priesthood continually to offer sacrifice – what the new covenant sees as 'a spiritual temple, a holy priesthood' is the entire covenant community whose perfect sacrifice has already been made by Christ. There can be no offering of baptism or eucharist to *atone* anew for man and, thus, there need be no sacrificing priesthood for such a task. The covenant community is the priesthood which offers sacrifices of obedience which it has been enabled to do by the atoning sacrifice already made. Those exercising priestly functions do so on behalf of the priestly community and, as representative priests, observe the sole criterion that they can assist the community to offer its sacrifice, be it baptismal or eucharistic. What makes Christians members of a priestly body is membership of the covenant, and what makes them members of the covenant is baptism. That this is no strange doctrine is made clear in the language of Vatican II's *Decree on the Ministry and Life of Priests* which calls baptism 'the symbol and gift of such a calling', i.e. that all Christians may work for the building up and care of the Church (*cf.*secs.7 & 12). Those who perform specifically priestly functions do so as pastors and liturgical presidents enabling the community to offer, no longer a sacrifice of atonement, but a sacrifice of obedience as befits the covenant. The question of who can function as a priest is solely the one of who is capable of carrying out the enabling functions and who will be recognised by the covenant community as its representative in the presidential role in such a manner as to bring peace, the characteristic of life in the covenant. Within that context lies the significance of the shift from Jesus's acknowledgement of the situation at the beginning of the old covenant, 'Have you never read that the Creator made them from the beginning male and female?' (Matt.19:4) to the position taken by Paul, 'Baptized into union with him . . . there is no such thing as Jew and Greek, slave and freeman, male and female' (Gal.3:28). The changed task of priesthood has changed the capacities and characteristics required.

The failure to understand this point is borne out by the failure to ask the question, Why, if entry to the covenant can be presided over by any baptised person, cannot any baptised person preside at the covenant's renewal? Unlike today, the early Church saw much debate over baptism but it was the issue of the validity of heretical or schismatic baptism which arose – Cyprian, Tertullian, Cyril of Jerusalem and Athanasius against it, with Augustine allowing its validity. The minister of baptism was less at issue. Tertullian asserted the right of the laity to baptise ('for what is received by all alike can be given by all alike' – a dictum of uncertain consequences) yet he would not have women do so. Ignatius went so far as to disallow baptism without the bishop's presence, but he may well have had in mind the whole rite of initiation. But when it comes to covenant renewal, the question of authority to preside suddenly becomes of paramount importance. When we recall that in the era of burning Reformation controversy, baptism tended to be a private rite, that the eucharist was by contrast the public assembly touching ordinary worshippers week by week, does it seem strange that the latter rite should attract all the attention? Besides, that is where the controversies over sacrifice were liturgically expressed.

On what principle are some to be chosen to preside, and others not? Jesus's choice was limited to start with by the impossibility of relating personally in the flesh to an infinite number and further limited by his choice of the symbolic twelve (the old Israel had twelve tribes). In any case, human nature demands that relationships start small, and there is also the point that the one redeems the few, and the few redeem the many. (The same principle applied to the attitude of Paul to marriages between Christians and pagans (1 Cor.7:14.)) The group of disciples and women were closely tied by kinship. Given the importance of the family in Judaism, and the place of women, it seems that the apostolic group can be accounted for by practical and cultural dictates. And when a successor was chosen for Judas, the early Church drew lots from those who met the essential criterion; being an eyewitness. Likewise, Paul chose local leaders for the churches from those persons having recognised authority and thus capable of representative presidency. Paul was himself chosen by Jesus as one capable of serving him – there is no evidence that the other apostles gave him his role.

The unwillingness of the Church of England to accept non-episcopally ordained ministers in the past is perfectly understandable – such persons had rejected the authority of an episcopal church and therefore Catholic order, and granting episcopal authorization for such a person to preside would be self-contradictory. But that is not the case with the Ten

Propositions; the churches are pledged to virtual absorption by the episcopal system – the only reason for not episcopally ordaining a particular person seems to be to avoid the invidious declaration that his previous presidency has been null and void. On the whole, covenant principles hold that the Church has the freedom to appoint whoever will be capable of functioning and whoever will be accepted by the community as a representative.

Reliability and Repetition

The signs of entry to both the old and new covenants are by nature unrepeatable: the former as an action impossible to repeat, the latter as an action needless to repeat. The once-for-all character of these rites arises from trust in the covenant's author that he will be true to his promise. Those who enter the covenant are never to be deserted and will never need to begin all over again. In baptism, the Christian has died to self and been raised with Christ in what is necessarily as unique an event as the passion and resurrection. When emphasis moves from the giver to the recipient, however, the sign stops speaking of God's dependability and instead murmurs about ever changing psychological and intellectual attitudes – unreliable like a house built on sand.

But men do alter. Not only do generations pass and new members are initiated but the covenant community's setting changes and the implications of membership have to be reassessed and reaffirmed. The purpose of passover was to bring the whole community, as well as individual members, to an ever new awareness of its identity as God's people, and the function of the eucharist is likewise both to feed the individual spirit and to renew the self-awareness of the community. If the unrepeatability of baptism allows it to bear witness to the permanence of the covenant, repetition of the eucharist allows the eucharist its role of re-forming the faithful community. Uniqueness and repetition are built into each respective sign. In baptism we receive the promise of the covenant and in the eucharist we are enabled to persevere during the interval between the promise and its fulfilment.

The intrusion of individualistic re-baptisms, 'baptisms in the Spirit', professions of new-found faith by the 'twice born' show a failure to grasp the witness of unrepeatability, as does the consideration of confirmation as a rite of growth. Aquinas's consideration of confirmation as a sacrament of growth, and Anglican elaboration of it as *the* rite of commitment, reveal failure to accord the two signs their proper status. Confirmation as the principle rite, either of growth or commitment, falls to the ground – the rite is not repeatable. The attempt to make a one-time rite do the work of a repeated rite can only lead to confusion. Unique events, like repeated ones, each have their own message to give. The covenant comes from God who, faithful to himself, does not annul his covenant at whim, nor at each infraction by its members. The existence of more than one covenant in the Old Testament meant restatements of God's promise to the changing community – no individual member entered more than what was for him *the* covenant. All the events of Christ's passion were steps in the one self-offering culminating in the cross. Entry to the paschal mystery is unrepeatable because, once having been entered, no possibility of restoration to a *status quo ante* exists in a relationship between persons. Man may look forward to righteousness but never again can he be in innocence. Because to enter the covenant is to enter a state of union with the paschal Lord, entry to the paschal mystery by baptism (which is another way of saying entry into the covenant) is no more capable of reverting to the condition of never having been a member than a wife can revert to virginity. Renewal of a relationship is, however, necessary if the beginning is to avoid, not cancellation (which is impossible), but going sour.

The Signs of Sacrifice

The signs of membership in a sacrificial covenant have sacrificial overtones. The new covenant springs from one who sacrificed himself for the sins of the world and membership is membership in a community nurtured by that sacrifice – it is unavoidable to call baptism sacrificial in that it implements the benefits of Christ's death, and to call the eucharist sacrificial since it commemorates that death. Yet the sacrificial nature of baptism has never provoked the controversy which eucharistic sacrifice has. Eucharistic sacrifice has, however, been taught in species-centred terms which raise the spectre of the altar emptying the cross of unique sacrificial content. Species-centred theology can do no other.

In the covenant, the main attribute of sacrifice is obedience: 'I will take no bullock out of thine house, nor he-goat out of thy foals . . . Offer unto God thanksgiving, and pay thy vows unto the most Highest.' (Ps.50:9 & 14). The Epistle to the Hebrews talks of the covenant responses of Abel, Enoch, Noah, Abraham, Sarah – sacrificial all of them – in terms of their faith (cap. 11). Few of them made a sacrifice in the popular sense but all of them were obedient. Obedience also lies at the heart of baptism and eucharist since the sacrifice of Christ was not a unique event in which we can have no part, but a willingness to obey in which we can share. Christ is our representative and perfecter, not our substitute. Not only do we obey in simply doing the rites of covenant membership, and hence sacrifice, but both rites are sacrificial in what they set forth and commend to worshippers. Circumcision required the sacrifice of obedience and signified it by submission to mutilation, baptism requires obedience to Christ and signifies it whilst incorporating us into the community established by his death; passover required an annual renewal of obedience and signified it by the eating of the prescribed sacrificial lamb, eucharist demands obedient renewal with confession and communion and signifies sacrifice by the sacrificial Lamb of God. But whereas species-centred sacramentalism raises stumbling-blocks to otherwise natural sacrificial connotations in the eucharist, the covenant relates the sacrifices of worshippers to that of Christ in a natural and biblical manner, *in terms of obedience:* both signs of the covenant are sacrificial because they relate to the sacrificial community's need for obedience.

While baptism and eucharist are not self-sufficient acts of atonement, they apply the benefits of Christ's atoning sacrifice and realise atonement by *anamnesis*, a concept that has roots deep in the history of the old covenant: Elijah visited the widow of Zarepath who said to him when her son fell ill, 'Have you come here to bring my sins to remembrance and kill my son?' A cause is realised, made present, through its consequences. Jesus's command, 'Do this in *anamnesis* (remembrance) of me,' makes contemporary his causative presence through its effects.

In that sense, the atonement is sacramentally present because the atoning Lord is present sacramentally. Since the atonement's benefits are applied in the two signs, they take the form of the obedient sacrifice which the covenant community offers. That which joins together the atonement and sacrifice in baptism and eucharist is the sacramental presence of the Lord in the midst of the covenant community. Light from a star many light years distant reach us so that we see the star of the past by ascertaining its light now – this analogy shows a past which becomes present without ceasing to be past.

Both baptism and eucharist are sacrifices in four respects. They are done by the covenant community as obedient acts. By these acts we belong to that community which only exists because of Christ's sacrifice. By these acts we draw on the sacrificial Lord and are given the help to obey him in the world where the covenant is observed. By these acts using water, bread and wine, we point to those elements in the world and see them as signs of his presence there, having been told by his word in scripture to look for him there – we obediently proclaim who is Lord of all, and who manifests his presence in the paschal signs.

The Presence of Christ

In the Exodus and Numbers accounts of Israel on the march in the time of Moses and Aaron, the priests had to exercise special care over the table of the presence of the Lord, a portable sign of the divine presence left to the people (Exod.25:23–30, Num.4:1–20). It was no cosy immanence, as the warning not to touch it lest they die, indicated. In the new covenant, Jesus promised his presence but applied it directly to presence in the covenant community – where two or three are met together in prayer (Matt.18:20) and among the gentiles to whom the covenant was extended (Col.1:27). That the eucharist is a sign of the presence is widely accepted, but baptism also signifies the presence of Christ as in the last words of Matthew's gospel, 'baptize men everywhere . . . and be assured, I am with you always, to the end of time'. The promise raises up hope because the Lord lives and it provides a foretaste of glory (Col.1:27). In Acts, the two disciples on the road to Emmaus recognised, in the breaking of the bread, Jesus's presence – they saw why their hearts had 'burned within' them. Jesus then showed the other disciples the marks of his cross, his hands and feet, and in eating (in this case a broiled fish) further manifested his presence. The liturgy parallels this event with the tokens of his body and 'blood' (his obedience unto death, his sacrifice) and the act of eating and drinking which also make known his presence in fulfilment of his promise (Lk.24:42). Scripture is the word which has elucidated and supported the signs of his presence – 'he began with Moses and all the prophets, and explained to them the passages which referred to himself in every part of the scriptures' (Acts 24:27). Words have given meaning to the bread and wine and the eating and focused attention on his presence yet words have been underrated by the traditional theology of signs. The medieval Roman mass's concentration on conversion of elements effected by words of institution tended to demote the liturgy into merely a framework designed to set off what really mattered – the miracle of conversion of elements. Ordinary Christians did not take themselves to be cannibals, however, and even the least articulate worshippers must have sensed that it was the divine person who was present. They made the jump from acknowledgement of body and blood to awareness of a personal presence, a jump neither necessitated nor accounted for by the conversion of elements. Aquinas knew what his successors did not always see – that a two-step signification was active: first the conversion of bread and wine into body and blood, then body and blood into the whole and living Christ. All eyes in Rome may have been fastened upon conversion into what was militantly asserted to be the true body and blood born of the Virgin Mary, and may have held that to be a declaration encapsulating almost the whole of what was worth proclaiming to be Catholic at that time, but we can see that discerning the body and blood is not the same as detecting Christ's personal presence. The missing ingredient in the spiritual alchemy is Christ's promise. Queen Elizabeth I had a point when she remarked,

Christ was the Word who spake it,
He took the bread and brake it,

And what that word doth make it,
That I believe and take it.

His words did what only words can do – they identified the meaning of what is on the table. The canon's reliance on his word was not so wide of the mark after all. In the last resort, species-centred liturgy relied at its most awesome and victorious moment not upon intrinsic meaning in the elements at all, but upon the words which designated, commanded, promised and signified: 'This is my body given for you . . . my blood of the (new) covenant shed for you and for many. Do this in remembrance of me.' If the 'miracle of the altar' distorted liturgy by ignoring its four-fold action of taking, blessing, breaking and giving, as Dix saw it, it did at least take Jesus's promise to heart. Even the four-fold action hangs upon Christ's promise. Liturgy which strays far from that promise becomes meaningless. The Series 3 revisers in England took seriously Dix's insistence on liturgy-as-action-not-words in writing a consecration prayer which drew out the idea of Real Presence and prolonged it over the entire continuum from sursum corda (which they re-worded to start 'The Lord is here. His Spirit is with us' just to emphasise the point) to Lord's Prayer, omitting all manual acts in connection with the words of institution. Separated from Jesus's promise, however, the actions fail to speak clearly of presence and so churches commonly observed an unrubrical concentration on the central words, usually accompanied by manual acts. The Alternative Service Book restores the old salutation in the sursum corda (while allowing manual acts) recognition that the experiment of presence acknowledged by actions alone, has failed? Covenant theology has no need to import a concept to expound Christ's presence – the words signalling Christ's presence are his own words of promise.

If the Lord's presence is a *sine qua non* of the eucharistic renewal of covenant, why is that presence not also acknowledged at the baptismal entry into the covenant? Christians have so tightly bound themselves to looking for change in elements that they have not been concerned with a real presence in baptism, by promise. Here, too, the word's role is determinative – Christ provided words pointing directly to the elements for the Church's eucharistic devotion to seize upon, but no words of Christ that we know referred to a change in the water of baptism. Species-centred teaching was never invoked to argue for a real presence in baptism, but the raw material is nevertheless in scripture. In coming up out of the water at his baptism, Jesus's sonship of his Father was made known (Matt.3:16) and the divine presence is where Jesus is ('he who sent me is with me, and has not left me to myself', Jn.8:29). Jesus touched on the theme of water and access to his presence, 'If anyone is thirsty let him come to me', and quotes 'Streams of living water shall flow out from within him' (Jn.7:38). St John understood Jesus to be speaking of the later outpouring of the Holy Spirit, but even that interpretation is germane because the Spirit is the agent of Christ's presence in the faithful and in their sacraments. The Apocalypse directly ties Jesus to living waters as their source and water becomes the place where God and the faithful meet, 'the Lamb will guide them to the springs . . . and God will wipe all tears from their eyes' (7:17). The use of water in the gospel narratives taps a rich vein – Peter comes to Jesus on water until lack of faith sinks him (Matt.14:28), a man bearing a pitcher of water is to lead the disciples to the upper room where they will find Jesus (Mk.14:13). The fourth gospel makes much of the flow of water from Jesus's side at the crucifixion (Jn.19:34) and if the blood has suggested the eucharist to the Church, the water suggests baptism – both elements in this case speak of Christ's presence: they flow from his body.

In the Johannine account of the Resurrection appearances to the disciples (20:19–29) we have clear references to the covenant. The characteristic quality of the covenant is peace (Num.25:12, Ps.122:6, Isa.9:7, 54:10, Ezek.34:25, Mal.2:5). The Lord who promised a covenant in his blood shows them the marks of his death and announces that peace which comes from the covenant on the 'first day' of the week, itself a day symbolising a new creation. He re-asserts the peace of his covenant to Thomas on the 'eighth day', itself an eschatological symbol of the covenant's fulfilment and the day of circumcision in the old covenant (Lev.12:3, cf. Lk.1:59, Acts 7:8, Phil.3:5). The power to absolve is bestowed and forgiveness is an attribute of the covenant's peace. A Christian of the first century might see that this peace was bestowed in his own baptism and re-asserted in absolution, a restoration of the baptismal state. It was further announced on the eighth day, the end of the passover renewal, when Thomas encountered the risen Christ bearing the wounds of his covenant, a parallel to the eucharistic renewal where the risen Christ appears, on the eighth day, with the signs of his covenant-creating body and blood.

Our typical baptism is more a rite carried out obediently than an occasion of awe and adoration. Unlike the eucharist, there is little sense of a presence to be worshipped. Ought not the baptismal rites be written to encourage the awareness of a real presence in the act of covenant entry? The ASB (1980) of the Church of England does give an introductory sentence to the Peace in the communion service and explicitly refers to baptism as the ground of our presence at the eucharist. But it is otherwise not tied to any proclamation of Christ's presence. No such cross-reference to the eucharist can be found in the baptismal service. That baptism entitles new Christians to receive communion hardly occurs to lifelong churchgoers, let alone those on the fringes. Nevertheless, if the two signs are related by the covenant, it follows that they are related as signs of Christ's presence. The arbitrary limitation of 'Suffer the little children to come to me, forbid them not' (Matt.19:14) to baptism does not do justice to the new covenant.

The Signs of Community

The covenant-created community shows its parent's traits and the signs of that community's constitution do also. Signs need community, not only to observe them, but to charge them with meaning. The community is created and renewed by grace and its signs of entry and renewal so state. It reflects the mystery of life-through-death and its signs signify the community's paschal nature. It lives on the strength of God's promise and the signs encourage hope in the faithful. It proclaims God's universal sovereignty and the signs point to the divine-human love in all creation which alone underlies whatsoever things are true, honest, just, pure, lovely and of good report (Phil.4:8). What the community is and does, the signs signify and effect. The signs relate the individual member to the covenant community and influence both. Circumcision marked membership in Israel and passover the renewal of the individual as well as the community; baptism conveys forgiveness to the individual and membership in the Church, while the eucharist feeds the Christian as it renews the Church.

We have already seen the need to relate the two signs to each other properly and that the failure to do so is likely to have important consequences. Unrelated to communion, baptism only mutters about potential membership and 'the Church of tomorrow' and the only promise is of some future adult status – membership as such will not indicate active grace but will be reduced to being a future reward. Baptism, unsupported by eucharist, seems to look for a universal community (particularly where few of the baptised are tied to the requirements of communicant status) but the undemanding and understanding of that community inhibits the sacrament from encouraging the baptised to seek the Lord with vigour. The unsupported eucharist, comprising only a small portion of the baptised, seems more a club than the large community constituted by baptism.

Unrelated to one another, the two membership signs reinforce the apparent existence of two communities, one the baptised and the other the communicants. The signs could relate to each other through the covenant from which they assume their meaning but traditional sacramental teaching is not covenant-based. The failing goes beyond mystery theology which tried to relate the signs through their participation in the paschal mystery but ignored communal issues except for hierarchical ones; it goes beyond species-centred theology which encouraged individualistic attitudes to the sacraments and ignored covenant even though the covenant was part of Jesus's words of institution of the eucharist; it goes back to the predominance of mystical-body theology which, unchecked by any powerful rival, played fast and loose with time in general and in particular with time and age demands for the realization of membership, and also with the boundaries of the Church, wavering between a universalism on the one side, where the Church means the whole human race and on the other side, a sectarian Church comprising the 'saved' (even pretentiously enrolling a castrated covenant theology in its service). The path of mystical-body doctrine via the sacraments, unchecked, led to schism not only between the churches of east and west, but leads to internal schism within each of the major western churches themselves.

Membership as a sign of grace is also put at risk as achievement is allowed to become a ground for membership. Consequences for liturgy, within which the signs are set, are naturally serious. The 'liturgy' is now taken to mean the eucharist and not a baptism-eucharist unity, the liturgy is turned into an adult affair where the witness of children and adults to each other is lost, and confusion is raised over what weight to put on individual comprehension and faith as requirements of belonging. A host of derived problems arises from the failure to relate the signs adequately.

One of these arose from Cranmer's attempt to hammer out a relationship between the two signs without a covenant theology to help him. He, like most Anglicans ever since, tried to relate them through confirmation. Accepting the medieval idea of confirmation as a rite of growth through the gift of the Holy Spirit by the laying on of the bishop's hands, he added in the 1549 prayer book a stipulation that confirmands be of the 'age of discretion' and be able to ratify for themselves what their godparents had promised at baptism. The rite was to be ministered as a defence against sin at the age when sin became a threat. The link with baptism was shown by the necessity to have been baptised before confirmation, the ratification of baptismal vows by the confirmand, and the recital of the baptismal creed (the 'apostles' creed'). The link with holy communion was made in requiring confirmation before communion (based on a rubric from pre-Reformation days which had been often ignored; in any case infants could be confirmed, as was Elizabeth I), and also by the need to be able to recite the ten commandments which formed the opening of Cranmer's communion rite as well. The title of the service in the 1662 book reinforced the 'age of discretion' note and the rationale for confirmation has remained largely unchanged in Anglicanism since, despite debates over what constitutes the age of discretion. Vatican II ordered the inclusion of baptismal vows in confirmation and moved the Roman Catholic church in the same direction.

In attempting to relate the two signs, a virtual third sacrament has been erected which, in the case of Anglicans looking to scripture for authority, is ironic. The American Episcopal prayer book included Acts 8:14–18 (Peter and John going to Samaria to lay hands on the newly baptised) in 1892, and the 1962 official report of the Diocese of New York was able to say

> *Confirmo*, in classical Latin means, 'to strengthen the courage to be' – that is what Confirmation is all about. Prayer and the laying on of hands by the chief pastor accomplishes this. This is the covenanted arrangement by which the Lord hath bound us.[7]

The stirring biblical-sounding language is all there but the substance is lacking. The 1948 Lambeth Conference had said plainly that the Spirit was given only once, but the New York report was constrained to say 'Confirmation is God's gift . . . of the particular grace of the Holy Spirit' (thus overlooking Lambeth's distinction between grace and the Spirit, as well).[8] Recent writers agree that no one knows just what confirmation does. In fact, the very need to elaborate a rationale for the episcopal role in Christian initiation arises entirely in the western churches from the early-medieval historical difficulty of reaching a bishop, combined with the reservation of confirmation to the bishop's person. A gap appeared between baptism and confirmation unknown in the early Church which encouraged theology to be written to justify confirmation in its now separated state, a situation which, owing to the use of episcopally-blessed oil by the baptising priest, never arose in the eastern churches. The scriptural foundation for a separate rationale is flimsy – Acts 8 can be accounted for on the grounds that the newly baptised were Samaritans and hence outcasts from Israel – and the temptation to conjure it all up is removed once the covenant relationship between baptism and eucharist is understood.

On the whole, Anglo-Catholics pressed for younger communions and early confirmation to cast the communion net widely, losing as few children as possible. Some Evangelicals accepted confirmation as a proper occasion for what really mattered – personal affirmation of faith – as the prerequisite for communion. In the first case, the Mason-Dix line has plumped for a third sacrament to provide access to communion through the Spirit's action, while in the second case personal affirmation of the gift of faith has been held up as the title to communicant status; in neither case is communion related directly to baptism nor does baptism entitle one to receive communion. Extremists in the first camp devalue baptism in favour of another rite untied to baptism, extremists in the second camp devalue baptism in favour of an act of commitment untied to baptism, either. To add to the confusion, we have some who would reunite baptism, confirmation and communion by denying the lot to infants. They would achieve a logical solution at the cost of an important witness to unearned grace – the great point of paedobaptism – ignoring the communal nature of the covenant. That the temptation to construct unscriptural, and in the end unworkable, solutions ought to be avoided is not removed by recognising the valuable service performed by a third sacrament – an uneasy coalition between Anglo-Catholics and Evangelicals. A recent ecumenical study put the point well, '"confirmation" is an ambiguous term which too easily obscures the truth that the eucharist is the necessary and proper communion of baptism.'[9] Even within Anglicanism itself the solution now appears absurd – in Iran diocese young children were of late treated according to the rules of their home diocese: young Americans could receive communion but the young English not!

The covenant community never was an organization formed out of isolated individuals receiving signs of membership. It always included classes of persons incapable by nature of comprehending the covenant and its signs, or prevented from receiving the signs, or both. For instance, the impossibility of females receiving circumcision did not serve to exclude them from the covenant and the importance of women in the Old Testament shows the value placed on their being members. Tertullian, Cyprian, and Augustine held that martyrs undergo a baptism of blood which takes the place of water baptism, and that martyrs are the life blood of the Church. At first glance, this fact seems to devalue the signs but it is an exception which proves the rule. The old covenant relied on the unquestioned necessity of women for the very existence of any community to justify considering them as members. In baptism, however, the Church had, in a rite familiar to Jewish proselytes, a means of explicity encompassing both sexes. The Church's integrity was well served by a sign which demanded no distinctions between male and female, bond or free. The Church made the most of this – martyrs remained unbaptised only if absolutely necessary. The pressure to baptise sprang from the requirements of community as well as from the desire to provide membership by sign.

Despite lack of evidence on the extent of infant baptism in the earliest days, we know that the very young's inclusion was both early and general. St Paul regarded the children of a Christian parent (and the non-Christian spouse of a Christian) as belonging to God even if unbaptised (1 Cor.7:14) and we do not know for certain whether the 'household baptisms' of Cor.1:16 included all the children – what is certain is the pressure for inclusion arising from personal relationships in community. Tertullian's objections to infant baptism in the North African church under pagan siege were lodged not against its validity but its advisability and he made allowance for emergency baptism of an infant in immanent danger of death. Reluctance to baptise infants arose from the prospect of persecution and the fear of committing post-baptismal sin – no one argued that infants should not be baptised because the sign would be meaningless nor that children were excluded by nature, and once the pressures of the Constantinian period had receded, infant baptism became the norm. When, in the fourth century, the ranks of the catechumenate were swelled by those postponing baptism (to reduce opportunity for sin after baptism), the 'mass of the catechumens' provided a place in the liturgy for those who, while not yet baptised were undeniably part of the covenant community. Unbaptised members seemed something unnatural, even an embarrassment, and pressure was constant to extend baptism. What underlay the preaching that infants must not be allowed to run the risk of dying unbaptised was no sudden unaccountable hardening of hearts or seizure of amnesia causing the faithful to forget all about a God of love, but was simply the recognition that children were an indispensable element of the covenant community, as of any continuing community. Their inclusion in either covenant was never ruled out because they could not 'understand' – even idiots can be Christians! Indifference to infant membership tells us more about lack of community awareness than it does about God. Children, women, martyrs and idiots are given the signs of membership as much for the Church's benefit, as for their own.

The issue is the witness of such classes, and particularly children. Jesus put a child (παιδίον, a little, dependent child) amidst them and said, 'Truly, I say to you, unless you turn and become like children, you will never enter the kingdom of heaven' (Matt.18:2–4). He did this for the sake of adults to whom he was talking. St John's Gospel sees the same point and puts it in a liturgical setting, 'There is a boy here who has five barley loaves and two fishes; but what is that among so many? . . . Then Jesus took the loaves (and the fishes), and they had as much as they wanted' (6:9–11). Paul used νήπιος, expressing child-like simplicity and ignorance, which he applied to adults – 'I, brethren, could not address you as spiritual men, but as men of the flesh, as babes in Christ' (1 Cor.3:1). In the first instances Jesus singled out the child's trust and hopefulness as traits for all aspirants to the kingdom, in the second the gifts of the child suffice, in the third child-like ignorance is a warning to the Church. In all instances, the child has something to tell the community and his witness is built into the community and is necessary for the community's integrity. Such things are to be learnt from the simple, not the learned and wise. That the Church has at least begun to grapple with the issues of liturgy and community in a new way appears in some remarks by the former chairman of the (Episcopal) diocese of Washington's Liturgical Commission:

It is now quite clear that this [i.e. initiation] is where we should have started in the first place, but historically we couldn't . . . . We first had to take the liturgy seriously. Then after we took the liturgy seriously, we had to look at 11 o'clock Sunday morning because that was the thing that was hurting. And then . . . we saw that the thing that really was missing was that those people there didn't know what they were doing or what they were committed to. And all the bread and wine in the world wasn't going to make the difference . . . And as I see it, the real problem that we're dealing with is, 'How do you build a community?'[10]

A key question for the building of Christian community has long been, how can those incapable of an explicit act of faith, yet who are necessary for the fulness of community, be made members of the covenant? The answer lies in the relationships between the theological virtues of faith, hope and love. In caring for the child, love is manifested and hope nurtured for both child and community. St Paul stated as much (1 Cor.13:13); where love and hope exist, faith will follow, for 'faith is the assurance of things hoped for' (Heb.11:3). Augustine took the same point, 'Wherefore there is no love without hope, no hope without love, and neither love nor hope without faith.'[11] Calvin, too, saw the point – hope 'invigorates faith again and again with perseverence'.[12] The modern writer Moltmann dwells on the same theme:

> If it is hope that maintains and upholds faith and keeps it moving on, if it is hope that draws the believer into the life of love, then it will also be hope that is the mobilizing and driving force of faith's thinking, of its knowledge of, and reflections on, human nature, history and society. Faith hopes in order to know what it believes.[13]

Relationships within a community, indeed the community's very being, requires a network of acts of faith appropriate to the character of the members. Moreover, in baptising infants, the community incorporates change writ large. Such change is the stuff of that gain-through-loss which the Church sees to be paschal. This enables the covenant community to comprehend its own nature, and its Lord's, seeing changeableness not as a scandal with which it cannot reckon, but as a sign of the passion. The inclusion of those who show the greatest changes in their development is particularly apt when the world is tempted to repudiate change, not knowing what to make of it. In this setting, for the Church to harp on 'commitment' is futile. It is an unpaschal yearning for arrival characteristics which, if allowed to intrude unduly into covenant principles of membership, threatens the covenant community's signification of its paschal Lord. Fastening upon explicit acts of faith as the sole indication of authentic commitment betrays a failure to appreciate the covenant's community relationships as these witness to Jesus Christ. An adult style of commitment is no more proper to the renewal of membership in eucharist than it is proper to the bestowal of membership in baptism. 'How do you build a community?' The bible suggests you start with children and bring them right in! The recognition of the covenant as a community phenomenon presses for the community's internal cohesion, and for properly related signs to defend that cohesiveness.

Not only do the signs combat internal schism when they are properly related to each other, but in setting forth the nature of the covenant they promote the ecumenical unity of Christians. For instance, some say the eucharist should be used to bring about unity, that it is a God-given tool to that end. Others say the eucharist can be used only to express unity and that (so they imply) offering communion to separated Christians is tantamount to papering over schism. Neither attitude appreciates the truth about the witness of the signs.

What is true of baptism must be true of eucharist. Christ has brought into being only one covenant community. Almost all the 'main line' churches but the Baptists agree that Christians already possess a baptismal unity. Vatican II said so plainly.[14] If entry to the one covenant has already been given in baptism, renewal of the unity in eucharist must follow. We cannot have it both ways – if there is baptismal unity, the eucharist *need* not create it; if there is not baptismal unity, the eucharist *cannot* create it. What about the questions of order, of ministry, of authority to preside at the eucharist? The questions imply that without agreement on those issues, there is insufficient unity for the celebration of the eucharist. But the unity that matters for eucharistic celebration is baptismal unity and there is no doubt in most Christian churches as to who has been validly baptised. If the eucharist is seen as the renewal of baptism, and both are seen as signs of membership in the covenant, then the covenant community is prior in importance to all such derived issues. As long as the covenant community regards a eucharistic celebration as its own, whoever presides does so validly. In the past it has been seen the other way round, but as the writer to the Hebrews remarks, 'a consecrating priest and those whom he consecrates are all of one stock' (2:11). The objections stem either from theories of priestly authority raised outside the consideration of covenant requirements (e.g. the pipeline theory of apostolic succession), or from theories about certain classes of people like women being, by nature, unable to preside. Such considerations fall outside the principles of covenant.

The covenant community is, of course, one body through time and this fact encourages some to think that the Church can choose only such presidents as would have been acceptable in the past. But this appears not to have been the case in the biblical history of the covenant. No priesthood existed in the patriarchal period and authority descended to the head of the family: Noah (Gen.8:20), Abraham (Gen.22:13), the sheik for his tribe (Exod.2:16), the prince for his people (Gen.14:18). On Mount Sinai, Moses was ordered to consecrate Aaron and his three sons to minister (Exod.28:1) and the tribe of Levi was chosen, eventually to be given charge of the services of the Tabernacle with only the sons of Aaron exercising the functions of priesthood. The priesthood's composition can be seen to have changed during the covenant's history and in that fact, as well as in the failure of Moses to make use of the existing separate class of priests, in favour of 'young men' and himself (Exod.24:4–8), we detect no operative principle that the existing composition had to be maintained to provide authentication of the descendant community. What we see is the selection of priests in the later community which allows it to see its continuity with the earlier one. In other words, those who were chosen were not perpetuated by successors to authenticate the descendant priesthood. Rather, it worked from the other end – priests were chosen by the existing community with the capacity to assure that community's recognition of itself as the authentic heirs. The supreme example is to be seen in Christ – a priest of the order of Melchizidek – whose order lies outside the conventional priesthood of Aaron and the Levites precisely to identify him as the Messiah, the sole faithful remnant of the old covenant. The continuity between Christ and the old covenant is assured by a discontinuity in the priesthood's line. Neither Paul nor Matthias fulfilled the trait of having been chosen as apostles by

Jesus in the flesh nor even by the Spirit at Pentecost – they served as persons capable of bearing witness to the priesthood of Christ. According to this principle, the Church is bound to authorise, not the presidency of those recognisable as priests by the first-century Church, but of those persons who can today be taken as signs of identity between present and past communities. The covenant community's choice of apt ministers and its inclusion of children, as of other classes of member, safeguards the historical integrity of the community while reinforcing recognition that the covenant is itself a sign of grace.

5

Worship and the Secular Order

We saw that mystery-body theology tends to view the world
pretentiously as a place to be subjugated, or irreverently as a
place where Christ is absent. What different things does the
covenant have to say about the world? First, the world shares
certain characteristics with the covenant. Like the covenant, it
has come into being, not by accident nor inner necessity, but
because of divine initiative and commitment. The world is not
simply a tragedy destined to destruction without issue. It was
created by a God whom the covenant people know to be both
redeemer and life-giver as well. Like the covenant, the world
bears paschal marks, it breathes life-through-death and in all
its life decay is found. The Dominican priest Roqueplo calls
this phenomenon 'paschal isomorphism' in which passion
marks are to be detected. A certain congruity exists between
cross-and-resurrection, seed-and-harvest, childhood's death-
and-adulthood's birth. Charles Raven, onetime Regius
Professor of Divinity at Cambridge, a naturalist of some
standing, knew that the marks of any living organism were
'adaptation to environment, growth through sensitive
adjustment, survival through changes of form'.[1] Karl Rahner
wrote of the temptation not to believe this is a paschal world:

> . . . when, in disillusionment, (man) faces reality as it is,
> when he is aware of and suffers from dead-ends and defeat
> and death as the tragedy of everything in the world and of
> all culture, all engaged in reducing itself *ad absurdum* – it is
> precisely then that he is subject to the most hideous of
> temptations: to regard the world as the tragedy of the
> meaningless.[2]

For him, such experiences are the cup of the world's passion,
the liturgy in the world's own peculiar form. Like the
covenant, the world is also a place of promise. Space men
strive to learn of places they know they themselves will never

73

reach. Human efforts which cannot possibly see personal realization in this lifetime are constantly made and they are not to be dismissed as foolish. Like the covenant, mankind manifests its own bias towards universality both in extending its dominion and in seeking brotherhood amongst all men. Covenant-like characteristics in the world point to a hidden presence. The Lord does not have to be taken there, he has gone before.

If these traits point to the Lord's presence in the covenant community, they do the same in the rest of creation. Matthew 25 plainly teaches such a presence in all mankind, 'Lord, when was it that we saw you hungry and fed you? Inasmuch as you did it to one of the least of these . . . you did it to me.' At the heart of the eucharistic prayer we find Jesus's words, 'this is my body given for you, my blood of the (new) covenant which is shed for many'. Roqueplo suggests we see these in a new light, turning towards a world of water, bread and wine, and communities. He speculates that Jesus spoke the words 'to reveal that bread was his body before he said it'. 'Was not the eucharistic institution the liturgical proclamation among believers of the universal existential sacrament offered to all men?'[3]

Water, bread and wine are properly called sacramental only if they mark Christ's presence and are means of grace. At the very least they depend for existence upon God who not only brings them into being but also maintains their continued existence; in a natural sense, as creatures, they signify their creator and sustainer. But more than that, they belong to the Redeemer and serve his purpose. To those with eyes to see, therefore, they are means of grace. Members of the covenant recognise the signs because their community values the elements as signs. In the same way, the elements can be recognised as signs of grace insofar as there exist communities which use water, bread and wine as instruments of care. Such caring has traits which, in its own life and according to its own terms, the covenant community knows to be paschal. Community is as essential for the recognition of the significance fo the elements in the world as the covenant community is essential for the recognition of Christ's presence by signs.

This truth ought to determine the attitude of the Church toward that world of signs in community within which the Church belongs and within which its covenant operates. Alas, the failure of Christians to appreciate the relationship between its signs and the covenant has led to equal failure to see the meaning of the world's communities, and their place in the economy of salvation.

The first step towards redressing the evaluation of the world has occurred in our era in the phenomenon of secularization. Secularization is a word which suggests the denial of a religious hegemony; it hints at rejection of a competitor striving to suppress the world's legitimate aspirations to understand the world 'in its own terms'. Christianity has tended to see the creation as two realms. Relations between the two realms were not always inimical but even when cordial there was a feeling that two different realms were to be related to each other. Richard Niebuhr analysed the experience of duality in *Christ and Culture*,[4] seeing five ways in which the two were related: Tertullian and Tolstoy related them so as to condemn the latter as a man-made evil; Abelard and Ritschl saw Christ as part of culture, the greatest achievement of a divinely inspired culture; Justin Martyr, Clement of Alexandria and Aquinas saw a synthetic relationship in which culture leads towards a Christ who is always above culture but who is revealed in reason and order; Paul and Marcion saw two moralities opposed; Augustine and Calvin had a conversionist view which looks towards the world's salvation through conversion to Christ. All these views shared a dual perspective and the advent of secularization represents nothing less than the rejection of ecclesiastical pretensions to universal jurisdiction which were the corollary to the unchecked mystical-body metaphor of the Church. As a result of that metaphor's sway over the Church's self-understanding, and because of that metaphor's inability to limit itself, the claims have been asserted with such vehemence that the secular realm's reaction has been militant as well. Ecclesiastical claims have a long history reaching high-points with the False Decretals and the Donation of Constantine and the Crusades and while, from time to time defeat has had to be admitted by Christians, the attempt to press such claims has never been systematically

75

repudiated by the Church. Realities of power have compelled soft-pedalling but in their hearts not a few Christians still believe that if only the world would surrender to the Church, or that if everybody were to belong to the Church, the world would be a much better place. Certainly the trimming of the Church's sails appears to many Christians to mean only the triumph of irreligion. Secularization is taken as a regrettable development they are unable to reverse.

Advocates of secularization have tended in the heat of the struggle to generate a hardening of purpose called secularism, a dogmatic rejection of religion. But even in the modern world there are cases where secularization has occurred without edging toward secularism. In Poland the Church is clearly the religious expression of, and partner to, the community identity of a whole people. This people has survived because of a strong commitment to language, culture and separate identity in the face of outside threats. The people persists because of a paschal experience in its own history. The Church as a covenant community provides the broad analogy on which the national life draws. No sharp line exists between Catholic life and Polish life. Malta presents a similar case. Secularization there is, but no formal organization into anti-religious secularism apart from what is imposed from outside and what is therefore a threat to being a people. Similarly, the Japanese do not fit into the duality; the Japanese even tried once to declare the state religion Shinto a non-religion! In no primitive African society do we find a sacred-secular opposition; things may be evil but not secular.

Though many are cold to the Church, people seem remarkably responsive to the person of Jesus, recognising an appeal in him which is not totally identified with, nor subsumed by, the mystical-body idea. Sensing that the person of Jesus, and the sort of communal relationships he did and does establish, have greater things to tell than the Church believes. The world undergoes its own passion and recognises kinship with Christ's passion. As Christians participate in his paschal mystery through membership in the covenant, people also participate in the worldly passion through membership in the world's communities, and above all in our time by entering into the yearning for one world, the need for which is now a

76

matter of human survival. But even if one paschal world community were acknowledged, it would not vindicate the unbridled claims of ecclesiastical imperialism. The world-wide paschal community would still bear at its heart the unrecognised Christ. Its life blood would be his gift of water, bread and wine, used in a community which his grace alone makes possible, but it would not be a Church. As to the travellers on the road to Emmaus, the stranger would perhaps be fleetingly recognised in the breaking of bread. He would be the one about whom the scriptures were written, but he would still vanish from sight. The Church would be the sign of Christ's presence, continually proclaiming the identity of the invisible figure who is seen only as reflected in 'the least of these'.

A covenant doctrine of Church and sacraments serves the Church in helping the covenant community serve the world Christ came to redeem. First, the covenant idea vigorously promotes the unity of the Church. It does this, not only by talking bible language to the churches but by insisting on each church's internal unity. The signs by which the Church is constituted and renewed are related to each other by their place in the membership pattern of one community – the community built round baptism must be the same as that built round eucharist. In other words, holy communion must be open to the baptised. To effect that, the two signs cannot be as they are now, separated by years, nor can confirmation be allowed to hinder free passage between the two signs. The only way to end the separation while retaining confirmation is to re-unite the baptism-confirmation-communion sequence as one event.

Should that event take place for infants or for adults? To answer that, we take into account the second task of a covenant theology – to promote membership as itself a sign of God's grace. The covenant community did not create itself and by its constitutive signs it must show as much. Achievement cannot be allowed to masquerade as the community's formative principle and that necessity suggests the way to undo the internal schism and symbolise unearned membership is to opt for child communion.

Covenant theology promotes better understanding of baptism and eucharist, seeing them as part of the covenant's constitution, and interprets each sign in relation to the other. Baptism is enriched to signify genuine, not proleptic, membership; eucharist is seen to provide access to Christ's humanity.

The covenant upholds the goal of union with Christ's human nature and, because it depends upon a mediator who is like us in all respects save sin, points to human relationships as the means of participation in the paschal mystery. Not only are the mediators human but so are the major covenant characters like Abraham and Noah. Once made, the covenant gives birth to a community which, united to its Lord, is clearly limited by human limitations and is easily distinguished from its Lord.

Covenant theology promotes a realistic but reverent attitude toward its environment, seeing it as a place with parallels to the covenant's signs which reveal it as a paschal place. The covenant signs of Christ's presence point to the Lord's presence in the world.

Finally, the covenant promotes a deeply biblical rationale for the Church and her two basic sacraments and compensates for the weaknesses of the mystical-body outlook. The signs of covenant membership are brought into line with bible teaching, and the restoration of child membership accords with the biblical understanding of the role of children in the Church.

Notes

Notes to Chapter 1

1. *La Maison-Dieu*, XIII (1948), p.7. (All translations from French are mine unless otherwise noted.)
2. Priests of St Séverin (Paris) and St Joseph (Nice), *What is the Liturgical Movement?* (London: Burns & Oates, 1964) Faith and Fact Book No. 110, trans. by L. Sheppard, *passim*.
3. From 1884 Maredsous published *Messager des fidèles*, from 1890 entitled *Revue Bénédictine*; in 1893 they also began publishing *Anectota Maredsolana*.
4. Carlo Falconi, *The Popes in the Twentieth Century* (London: Weidenfeld & Nicolson, 1967), *passim*.
5. Charles Davis, *Liturgy and Doctrine, the Doctrinal Basis of the Liturgical Movement* (New York & London: Sheed & Ward, 1960), p.11.
6. Hans Küng, *Structures of the Church* (London: Burns & Oates, 1965), trans. by S. Attanasio, p.321.
7. Falconi, *op. cit.*, p.288.
8. For a discussion of these abortive reforms, cf. Koenker, *The Liturgical Renaissance in the Roman Catholic Church* (Univ. of Chicago Press, 1954), pp.21–26; Reinhold in *Orate Fratres*, XXI (1946–47), 513; F. Heiler, *Katholizismus, seine Idee und seine Erscheinung* (München: Verlag von Reinhardt, 1923), pp.652–53.
9. *La Maison-Dieu*, XIII (1948), 12.
10. Para. 92.
11. *Summa Theologica*, IIIa pars, qu. 63.
12. An appreciation of Beauduin in A. Haquin, *Dom Lambert Beauduin et le renouveau liturgique* (Gembloux: Editions J. Duculot, S.A., 1970), p.221.
13. W.H. Frere, *Some Principles of Prayer Book Reform, a Contribution Towards the Revision of the Book of Common Prayer* (London: John Murray, 1911).
14. *Liturgy and Society, the Function of the Church in the Modern World* (London: Faber & Faber Ltd, 1961), *passim*.
15. For information about Hoskyns and Cobham, I am indebted to Archdeacon Cobham's letters to me of 26 November 1971 and 29 May 1972.
16. Filmstrip 1202, *Towards a Patristic Ceremonial* (with an introduction by Cobham).
17. It is Cobham's impression that the first of the Cambridge colleges with the arrangement of matins and eucharist described, was Corpus Christi.

Notes to Chapter 2

1. Odo Casel, *The Mystery of Christian Worship, and other Writings* (Philadelphia: The Westminster Press, 1962) Ed. by B. Neunheuser, p.6.
2. *Cf.* E. Masure, *The Sacrifice of the Mystical Body* (London: Burns Oates, 1954) Trans. from French original of 1950 by A. Thorold, p.8 fn.
3. E. Schillebeeckx, *Christ the Sacrament of Encounter with God* (London & Melbourne: Sheed & Ward Stagbooks, 1963) Trans. from original of 1960, p.65.
4. *Mediator Dei* (1947), para. 173.
5. A. Vonier, *A Key to the Doctrine of the Eucharist* (London: Burns Oates & Washburne Ltd, 1925), p.20.
6. T. Filthaut, *La Théologie des mystères: exposé de la controverse* (Paris: Desclée & Cie; 1954) Trans. from German original of 1947 by J.-C. Didier & A. Liefooghe, p.41 quoting Casel.
7. F.W. Dillistone, *The Structure of the Divine Society* (Woking & London: Unwin Press Ltd, 1951), p.183.
8. *Cf.* 1 Cor 11:29.
9. *26th Tract on John*, quoted in M.C. D'Arcy, *Selected Writings of St. Thomas Aquinas* (New York: E.P. Dutton & Co., Inc; 1950), p.43.
10. L. Bouyer, *The Paschal Mystery: Meditations on the Last Three Days of Holy Week* (London: Geo. Allen & Unwin Ltd, 1950) First pub. by Paris: Editions du Cerf, 1947; Trans. by M. Benoit, pp.118 & 119.
11. *The Shape of the Liturgy* (Westminster: Dacre Press, 1945), p.630.
12. *Institutes*, IV.xiv.1, in H.T. Kerr, Jr.(ed.), *A Compend of the Institutes of the Christian Religion by John Calvin* (Philadelphia: Presbyterian Board of Christian Education, 1939), p. 185.
13. For a discussion of this whole issue see Cyril C. Richardson, *Zwingli and Cranmer on the Eucharist, Cranmer dixit et contradixit* (Evanston, Ill.: Seabury-Western Theol. Sem'y, 1949), 57 pp.
14. *Revelation of the Father*, p.40 cited in J.F. Bethune-Baker, *An Introduction to the Early History of Christian Doctrine to the Time of the Council of Chalcedon* (London: Methuen & Co. Ltd, 1903), p.31, fn.
15. *The Body of Christ*, cited in Bethune-Baker, *op. cit.*, p.31, fn.
16. *Cf.* Priests of St. Séverin etc, *op. cit.*, Part II, *passim*.
17. *Op. cit.*, p.114.
18. See M. Thurian, *The Eucharistic Memorial* (London: Lutterworth Press, 1960), Trans. by J.G. Davies.
19. So maintained D.M. Paton, *The Parish Communion To-day* (London: SPCK, 1962), p.108.
20. J.M. Barkley, *The Worship of the Reformed Church* (London: Lutterworth Press, 1966), p.60.

Notes to Chapter 3

1. J.G. Davies, *The Spirit, the Church and the Sacraments* (Westminster: The Faith Press, 1954), p.46.
2. Gerhard von Rad, *Old Testament Theology* (London: Oliver & Boyd), I (1962), pp.129 *et seq.*
3. J.G. Davies, *op. cit.*, p.43.
4. T.C. Vriezen, *An Outline of Old Testament Theology* (Oxford: Basil Blackwell, 1958), p.142.
5. *Ibid.*, p.140.
6. *Inst.* 2.10.4.
7. P. Parsch, *The Liturgy of the Mass* (London: B. Herder, 1957) Trans. by H.E. Winstone (3rd ed.), pp.5 & 13.
8. *Cf.* Dillistone, *op. cit.*, p.71.
9. *Dogmatic constitution on Divine Revelation*, para. 3; *Dogmatic Constitution on the Church*, para. 2.
10. *Dog. Const. on Div. Rev.*, para. 16.
11. *Constitution on the Sacred Liturgy*, para. 10.
12. E. Schillebeeckx, *The Eucharist* (New York: Sheed & Ward, 1968) Trans. by N.D. Smith, p.127.
13. Isaiah 54:10, *cf.* Ps. 111:5.
14. *Comm. in Matt 24:36*, C.R. 73, 672, cited in Van Buren, *Christ in Our Place, The Substitutionary Character of Calvin's Doctrine of Reconciliation* (London & Edinburgh: Oliver & Boyd, 1957), pp. 12 & 13.
15. Von Rad, *op. cit.*, II [1965], p.416.
16. J.G. Davies, *op. cit.*, pp. 46 & 47 who cites the study of W.J. Phthian-Adams, *The People and the Presence* (1942), p. 17.
17. The Nature and Destiny of Man: a Christian Interpretation (London: Nisbet & Co. Ltd., 1941), Vol. I (*Human Nature*), p.201 fn.

Notes to Chapter 4

1. J.G. Davies, *op. cit.*, p.125. *Cf. ibid.*, pp. 91, 92 & 125 *et seq.*
2. *Ibid.*, p.90; *cf.* Ephes.4:30.
3. Thurian, *op. cit.*, I, p.33.
4. J.G. Davies, *loc. cit.*
5. *A Review of the Doctrine of the Eucharist with Four Charges to the Clergy of Middlesex Connected with the same Subject* (Oxford: Clarendon Press, 1896), p.337.
6. David Tripp, *The Renewal of the Covenant in the Methodist Tradition* (London: Epworth Press, 1969), p. 51.
7. New York, Diocese of, *Ready and Desirous, Being the Report of the Commission on Preparation for Confirmation of the Diocese of New York 1958-62* (New York: Morehouse-Barlow Co., 1962), p. 14.
8. *Ibid.*, p.17.

9. N. Clark & R.C.D. Jasper (eds.), *Initiation and Eucharist: Essays on their Structure by the Joint Liturgical Group* (London: SPCK, 1972), p.14.
10. *Christian Initiation* (Associated Parishes: Pub. No.2, 1970), p.14.
11. *Enchiridion*, cap. VIII, cited in M. Dods (ed.), *The Works of Aurelius Augustine, Bishop of Hippo* (Edinburgh: T. & T. Clark, 1873), IX, 180.
12. Inst. III.2.42.
13. J. Moltmann, *Theology of Hope; On the Ground and the Implications of a Christian Eschatology* (London: SCM Press, 1967), p.33.
14. *Decree on Ecumenism*, 22.

Notes to Chapter 5

1. Quoted in F.W. Dillistone, *Charles Raven: Naturalist, Historian, Theologian* (London: Hodder & Stoughton, 1975), p.264.
2. *The Christian Commitment* (London & Sydney: Sheed & Ward, 1963), Vol. I, p.85.
3. *Expérience du monde, expérience de Dieu? Recherches théologiques sur la signification divine des activitiés humaines* (Paris: Les Editions de Cerf, 1968), p.194. Trans. mine.
4. (London: Faber & Faber Ltd, 1952), esp. pp. 53 *et seq.*

DATE DUE